Superior Memory

Superior Memory

John Wilding and Elizabeth Valentine

*Department of Psychology,
Royal Holloway, University of London, U.K.*

Psychology Press
a member of the Taylor & Francis group

Copyright © 1997 by Psychology Press Ltd., a member of the Taylor
& Francis group

Psychology Press
27 Church Road
Hove
East Sussex, BN3 2FA
UK

British Library Cataloguing in Publication Data

A catalogue record for this book is available from the British Library.

ISBN 0–86377–456–3 (hbk)
ISSN 0959–4779

Typeset by Acorn Bookwork, Salisbury, Wiltshire
Printed and bound in the United Kingdom by Biddles Ltd.,
Guildford and King's Lynn

Contents

Acknowledgements   vii

1. **What is Superior Memory?**   1
   Feats of Memory   1
   Varieties of Memory—Natural and Acquired   6
   Objectives of This Monograph   7

2. **Previous Studies of Superior Memory**   9
   Early Studies   9
   Later Studies   21
   Conclusions   54

3. **The Nature and Nurture of Memory**   55
   Training or Talent?   55
   Memory—One System or Many?   61
   Relations between Memory and Other Psychological Constructs   73

4. **The Search for Superior Memories: Is Anyone Out There?**   85
   The Tasks   87
   The Control Group   95
   First Study: 10 Subjects Claiming Superior Memory Ability   98
   Two Unusual Individuals   101
   Overview   114

5. **Memory Champions**   117
   The Subjects   119
   Results   121
   Discussion   133
   Strategists vs. Naturals   136
   Conclusions   141

6. **General Memory Ability and Forgetting—Evidence from the Group Data**   143
   Factor Analysis   146
   Conclusions   149

7. **Conclusions**   151
   Specificity of Superior Memory and Reasons for such Specificity   151
   General Features of Good Techniques   155
   General Natural Memory Ability   155
   Conclusions on Specific and General Memory Ability   158
   Memory Ability of Close Relatives and Early Awareness of Superior Memory Ability   159
   Relations between Autobiographical Memory and Memory Ability in Laboratory Tasks   159

Memory and Intelligence   159
Memory and Imagery   160
Final Thoughts   161

References   163

Appendix   172

Author Index   173

Subject Index   177

Acknowledgements

Thanks are due first and foremost to all our subjects, who have given freely of their time and contributed many insights about their memory abilities. Our colleagues and other researchers have contributed data, put us in touch with potential subjects and answered questions about their own work. We would particularly thank (in alphabetical order): Tony Buzan, Steve Ceci, Susan Cook, Peter Fitzgerald, Paul Gordon, Doug Herrmann, Mort Herrold, Ian Hunter, Peter Marshall, Charles Thompson, John Valentine, and Semir Zeki. We also thank the reviewers of the original manuscript for their helpful comments.

We are grateful to Hannah Lewis for drawing the pictures of Hitler and "Rowan", and to Mark Wells for help with other illustrations.

The work described in Chapter 4 was partly supported by the Central Research Fund of the University of London.

1

What is Superior Memory?

FEATS OF MEMORY

At the Second World Memory Championships held in London in the summer of 1993, many outstanding feats of memory were performed. Perhaps the most impressive was that of Dominic O'Brien, the eventual World Champion, who recalled 1002 randomly generated binary digits after half an hour's study. The next best performer recalled only 600 digits! O'Brien also correctly recalled 100 randomly ordered digits spoken at the rate of one every two seconds on two out of three tests; the organisers of the competition had devised this as a task on which they assumed the maximum score was beyond the capacity of any of the competitors! In another task, Jonathan Hancock, who came second overall in the competition and who was the winner of the Championship of 1994, memorised 100 names to faces correctly after 15 minutes' study.

This book is about unusual memory performances such as these and the people who produce them. What level of memory performance can human beings at their best achieve? How are such feats achieved? What do the findings tell us about memory in general? Researchers have often tended to turn to cases of memory impairment to answer questions about the structure and processes that underlie memory, but we believe that as much or more can be learned from studying exceptional memory performance and that exceptional performances raise many questions that tend to be neglected in the study of more normal memory abilities.

1

First, we will describe a few more examples of unusual memory, to illustrate the variety of ways in which superiority may be demonstrated, and we will consider what memory feats are popularly regarded as typical of someone with a good memory. Then we will draw out some of the problems and questions, which we will attempt to answer through a more systematic examination of the available evidence.

One of the oldest recorded feats of memory occurs in a story told by Cicero about the Greek poet Simonides, who was dining one day and reciting at a banquet. The roof later fell in and killed most of the assembled company, rendering their mangled bodies unrecognisable. Simonides escaped because he had been called away, and he was able to recall who had been sitting at each place in the banquet, so that the grieving relatives could each be given the correct body for the funeral rites. It seems from Cicero's account that this was an example of incidental learning and, though the number of guests and hence the magnitude of the achievement is not recorded, Cicero says that it convinced Simonides of the efficacy of the method of loci (placing images of material to be remembered in a physical location) and he subsequently developed it as a deliberate memory method.

Epic poets are well-known for their ability to recite poems of enormous length telling the history of the nation's heroes. This illustrates the importance of memory in cultures that depend on oral tradition for preserving information important to the community, such as flora, fauna, genealogies, and navigation routes. Studies of modern equivalents of these story tellers have shown that their recitations are not identical each time. Rather, the reciters "composed their songs anew on each occasion" (Lord, 1960). They had available *themes* covering recurring events, which might be made up of different combinations of *formulae*, smaller units describing specific incidents. The precise selection of formulae depended on the current mood and nuances of the situation being described. Examination of *The Iliad* or *The Odyssey* soon reveals that quite long standard descriptions of extended, recurring events are used many times throughout the poems, as well as smaller standardised fragments. Hence, rote learning is combined with other processes to produce the larger whole.

Rubin (1995) reinforces these conclusions in a recent detailed examination of oral traditions. He argues that what is handed down is a theme, not a verbatim memory; but multiple constraints determine stability without forcing the exact form of the text. These constraints also cue memory. They include organisation of meaning (obviously) and imagery, but sound patterns are equally important, especially rhythm, and also poetic devices such as rhyme and alliteration.

A rather different example of precise exceptional memory is that of the Shass Pollak, reported by Stratton (1982). These students of the

Talmud could recall where each word appeared on the page of 12 volumes of text!

Turning to some examples of individual feats, which have been recorded in more detail, the famous Russian memory man Shereshevskii (S for short), whose memory was described in detail by the Russian psychologist Luria (1975), demonstrated many remarkable feats. One of the most impressive was his recall of the following complex arbitrary mathematical formula after only seven minutes' study.

$$N . \sqrt{d^2 \times \frac{85}{vx}} . 3 \sqrt{\frac{276^2 . 86x}{n^2 v . \pi 264}} \, n^2 b \; = \; sv \, \frac{1624}{32^2} . r^2 s$$

Fifteen years later he could recall in detail, without warning, the method he had used to code the formula. Luria (1975, p. 43) implies that he also recalled the formula itself but is not explicit on this point. The method used was to turn the arbitrary symbols into meaningful people and objects: "Neiman (N) came out and jabbed the ground with his cane (.)." The number 3 with the square root sign was a large tree with three jackdaws in it, x was a stranger in a black mantle, and so on.

Aitken (Hunter, 1977) was a mathematics professor who demonstrated unusual memory ability, as well as extraordinary mathematical talent. One of his most impressive feats was to reproduce from memory the names and regimental numbers of an entire platoon of 39 men without apparently having made any deliberate attempt to learn them or having any expectation that such recall would be needed.

A favourite activity of those wishing to demonstrate impressive feats of memory is to learn vast sequences of the digits of pi. In 1981, Rajan Srinivasan Mahadevan recited 31,811 such digits in 3 hours 49 minutes (including 65 minutes of breaks). In 1987, Hideaki Tomoyori outdid this by reciting 40,000 digits, but he took 17 hours 21 minutes, including 255 minutes of breaks, so he worked much more slowly. Compared with this, the feat of Philip Bond when tested by us seems modest. He memorised a 6 × 8 number matrix in five minutes and eight seconds (several of our subjects were faster), but was also able to recall it perfectly two months later. No other subject we have tested has matched this.

The tasks we have presented in our own studies of memory have been less demanding than the examples given above, but they have nevertheless sometimes produced individual performances unmatched by any of the other experts we tested, as in the example just given. Another example occurred with the task of recalling the correct names to 13 faces (each face–name pair being presented for only 10 seconds). Several subjects who use special methods have been able to recall all 13 names when tested immediately. The mean number recalled by those who have "normal" memories and use no special methods is only between 3 and 4 (see Chapter 4). The really demanding test, however, is to recall the names to the faces when they are shown without warning a week later. Few people recall more than a solitary name, and even the expert memorisers do little better than this. However, one of our subjects, JR, having recalled 12 names on the immediate recall test, could still recall all of them a week later. The performance of our control group of "normal" memorisers indicated that this feat would only occur by chance once in ten thousand million times! Moreover, JR claimed to have no special method for this astonishing achievement.

Anecdotes of extraordinary feats of memory demonstrated by experts in particular fields, such as music and chess, are legion. The conductor Zander, at a talk given at the Third World Memory Championships, recounted two such stories. As an 11-year-old the young Saint-Saens offered to play any one of Beethoven's 32 piano sonatas from memory as an encore at a public performance. Toscanini once conducted the whole of the opera *Aida* from memory, having been called out of the orchestra at short notice; his eyesight was not adequate to reading the score.

These different feats are impressive for different reasons. Some demonstrate unusual ability to remember material where there is no indication of deliberate intention to learn (Simonides, Aitken); some impress by the sheer quantity of material which has been acquired by persistent effort (epic poetry, music, pi). It is quite likely that, in these cases, learning was faster than it would be in the majority of people attempting such a feat, if only because most people would surely find the task too slow and unrewarding to persist. However, usually no direct evidence is available on this point, so it remains unclear whether the feats should be attributed to superior memory ability as well as superior motivation and persistence. Hence, individuals with a wide knowledge of a particular type of material, especially when this is an unusual type, are impressive, but without adequate control of the conditions in which that knowledge was acquired, no conclusion can be drawn on their memory ability. Other cases, which demonstrate remarkable speed of acquisition or acquisition of an unusual amount of material in a controlled period (O'Brien's binary digits, S's formula, JR's names), do demonstrate superior memory ability. The last two of these cases also meet a second major criterion for superior memory ability, namely unusually accurate long-term retention.

These then are the three criteria which will be used in this book when evaluating memory ability: (1) rapid acquisition of material or (2) acquisition of an unusually large quantity of material in a measured time, and (3) long-term retention of an unusually large quantity of material acquired under controlled conditions. The first two criteria exemplify superiority mainly in encoding processes and the third exemplifies superiority in retention. Superiority in retrieval ability may be a further distinct ability, but the available data are simply inadequate for evaluating this possibility.

As has been demonstrated, unusual memory ability has been shown in very many different ways and there is no certainty that excellence in one type of performance will guarantee excellence in all. One of the questions that will recur throughout this book concerns the generality of superior memory performance, over different types of memory task, different types of material, and different components of the overall memory process. Answering this question obviously requires more systematic data than are provided by isolated examples of unusual memory from different individuals.

Many of the examples given earlier involve deliberate learning of sequences of symbolic material (especially digits), rather than retention of the type of information that is the original raw material of everyday memory processes (objects, their use and value, routes, or individual characteristics such as facial features). There must be some doubt, therefore, about how far it is possible to draw conclusions about more "natural" memory abilities from studies of deliberate learning of very specific types of material. Since one of the central topics of this book will be individual differences in natural memory ability and their relation to wider aspects of cognitive performance, such issues will arise frequently in ensuing discussions.

It is perhaps significant that recognition memory for pictures is extraordinarily good even in non-expert subjects (Shepard, 1967; Standing, Conezio, & Haber, 1970), while memory for numbers is normally equally strikingly bad. What is more, memory for naturally encountered features of the environment is often based on incidental learning during a single exposure while carrying on other activities, whereas memory for material such as numbers most often depends on deliberate intent and strategy. The less natural the material, the greater the need for deliberate and special methods to achieve good memorisation. In such cases, unusually good performance tends to be rare and people are more impressed by it. So memory for long strings of numbers is more astonishing than ability to reproduce music or chess moves, and these abilities are in turn more impressive than memory for poetry or people's faces or a series of events. There is, therefore, no guarantee that the person who has mastered the art of memorising long strings of digits has a good memory for where their car was parked in a strange town or where a particular face was previously seen.

Clever strategies can be very successful and can tell us a great deal about some aspects of memory function, but they are not, in general, necessary for everyday tasks and may not, without careful analysis, provide direct insights into the more automatic functioning of the memory system in everyday life.

VARIETIES OF MEMORY—NATURAL AND ACQUIRED

When we appealed on the radio a few years ago for volunteers with good memories whom we could test, we received a wide variety of replies, claiming a variety of accomplishments. However, there were a number of common themes, which suggested that people usually regard themselves and others as having a good memory for one or more of the following reasons.

1. They can remember and retell many events from their own life, especially from their early life.
2. They can relate stories, poetry, jokes, etc. accurately and vividly.
3. They remember individuals, particularly faces, names, and important biographical information.
4. They can remember a large number of facts, either of general knowledge or from some specialist field (one of our respondents had memorised railway timetables).
5. They remember routes of journeys.
6. They have a so-called "photographic" memory, which stores an accurate image of visual inputs (more of this dubious claim later).
7. They remember to do what they have planned to do.

These kinds of memory achievement are demonstrated in the situations for which memory evolved. Humans and other animals need to remember what happened in a particular situation so that they know what to do or what not to do next time it occurs; they need to remember characteristics of objects, including individuals of their own species; they need to remember the way back to the cave or a source of food; they need to persist in pursuit of a goal. Originally the individual with a better memory for these types of information would have had a better chance of survival. Once language developed, it became important to be able to encode and store experience in symbolic form and pass it on to others. Development of culture opened up other challenges to memory— retaining symbolic information communicated by others, tales and poems to pass on, dance routines, songs, and rituals, which required verbal, musical, and motor memory. However, these skills were a less direct product of evolution and were acquired by training rather than through genetic endowment. The development of writing rendered oral memory much less important, so such skills are now rarer in our society and thereby more impressive. More recently still, the advent of computer-based information systems, which permit storage and ready retrieval of huge amounts of information, is making oral memory still less important.

The main point that emerges from this discussion is that many of the most striking feats of memory performances such as those described earlier are not due to greater efficiency in an individual's natural memory but to the application of learned methods of memorising to large quantities of symbolic material, especially unstructured symbolic material. Consequently, these demonstrations may tell us more about ways of improving some aspects of memory by deliberately learned methods than about natural automatic memory capacities and methods of improving the latter.

OBJECTIVES OF THIS MONOGRAPH

The object of this monograph is to examine the evidence on superior memory performance in order to determine the factors that produce such performance and to consider the implications for theories of memory in general. In pursuit of this objective, the following are the main questions which will need to be examined.

1. Is superior memory performance typically *general* or *specific*—does it occur over a wide range of tasks or only in specific types of task?
2. If superiority is specific, is this due to a *technique* applicable to a particular type of task, or to a *specialised memory system*?
3. What characterises *successful techniques* and can they be learned by anyone? Does the practice of techniques have effects on general memory efficiency?
4. Does *naturally outstanding memory ability* occur? Is it general or is it specific to certain tasks, materials, or processes? On what does it depend? Is it qualitatively different from normal memory ability or just "more of the same"? How early in life is it apparent? Does it run in families? Is it characterised by good autobiographical memory, such as memory for early events in life?
5. What are the relations between *memory* and *other cognitive abilities*?

The reasons for undertaking a study of superior memory performance are not simply curiosity about unusual abilities, but a belief that a better understanding of memory processes and possible memory theories can be developed from such studies. To date, general studies of individual differences in memory have not been highly revealing in relation to such questions, compared with the study of individual differences in intelligence, for example. Examining exceptional cases may enable a clearer picture to be developed of the extent to which variation in memory abilities is general or specific, the extent to which different proposed types of memory are independent of each other, the separability of different component processes, and other related questions.

Chapter 2 will describe studies of superior memory performance carried out by other investigators and our own initial investigations of the subject TE. Chapter 3 will consider the above questions in the light of the evidence surveyed in Chapter 2 and will also consider a much wider body of evidence relevant to questions about nature versus nurture in memory efficiency, the specificity of memory systems, and relations between memory and other cognitive processes. Chapter 4 reports our examination of the claims to superior memory of a volunteer sample recruited following a radio broadcast and of two other exceptional subjects, employing a more extensive battery of tests than was used in the study of TE. Chapter 5 reports a study of contestants at the First World Memory Championships, leading to a distinction between strategic and natural superior memory. In Chapter 6 the results of a factor analysis of all the data accumulated during the course of our studies are reported and the implications of the results for theories of the structure of memory are considered. In the final chapter we return to the questions posed earlier and examine them in the light of the evidence we have accumulated, assessing the implications for future research.

2 Previous Studies of Superior Memory

The purpose of this chapter is to describe the evidence from cases of superior memory up to and including our own study of the mnemonist TE. The earliest evidence drawn from individual case studies is often fragmentary and anecdotal. Consequently only tentative answers can be given to the questions raised at the end of Chapter 1 on the basis of this evidence. We will, however, hazard provisional answers to those questions in relation to each case, leaving more systematic discussion till later.

EARLY STUDIES

There are many anecdotal accounts of individuals with superior memory. While these are interesting, they do not provide sufficiently reliable or detailed evidence to permit progress in answering the key questions raised in Chapter 1. There are also detailed early accounts of methods designed to improve memory, which encapsulate the essentials of virtually all the effective techniques employed by modern memory experts. Aristotle in his *Parva Naturalia* refers to the method of loci: "Some people seem, in recollecting, to proceed from *loci*. The reason for this is that they pass rapidly from one step to the next; for instance from milk to white, from white to air" (1957 edition, p. 305). For other discussions see the treatise by an unknown author entitled *Rhetorica ad Herennium* (Achard, 1989), Quintilian's *Institutio Oratoria* (1921–1922 edition), Cicero's *De Oratore* (1942 edition), and especially Yates, *The Art of Memory* (1966), for a readable account.

O'Brien (1993) briefly outlines what is known of 12 famous memory men, ranging from the first century B.C. to modern times. (Though all these cases are male, superior memory is not restricted to males, as our own data will demonstrate, but men have been more likely than women to perform as mnemonists, especially in competitive situations.) Three of these subjects (S, VP, Aitken), who have been studied with more scientific rigour, are discussed in detail later in this chapter. Barlow (1951) describes a large number of arithmetical calculators, many of whom also had superior memory for numbers, together with prodigies in the areas of chess, music, and memorising. Most of the accounts are brief and anecdotal, but they include some interesting examples. Jedediah Buxton (1702–1772) was a man of little intelligence with an amazing memory for numbers and impressive calculating ability. He once squared mentally a 39-digit number in two and a half months, carrying all the information in his head. Ampère (1775–1836) in his youth read through a 20-volume encyclopaedia and is said to have been able to repeat long passages on varied topics with perfect accuracy 50 years later. Mathematicians such as Gauss and Euler had remarkable memory for numbers. In a different field, an entertainer known as Datas used to move around Britain and do stage performances at the beginning of the present century, in which he would answer factual questions invited from the audience on any topic of historical or public interest. He would acquire local information by reading the local newspaper and talking to people in the local bars, then visualising pictures and connections between the facts he heard (as reported in his 1904 book *Memory by Datas: A simple system of memory training*). It was claimed that he never forgot anything he had ever heard or read. A more recent example of a similar nature is Leslie Welch, who showed a prodigious memory for sporting information on radio, television, and stage shows. Donald Francis Tovey is said to have had a remarkable memory for musical and other material (Grierson, 1952) but no detailed examples are provided.

Hunter (1990) describes in more detail three individuals, an American called K who was studied by Jones (1926), Leslie Welch (mentioned previously), and the historian Thomas Macaulay. Hunter highlights the differences between these three individuals.

K had a measured IQ in only the upper 70s but was obsessed by numerical information, which he absorbed like a sponge and recorded in detailed notebooks. This enabled him to earn a respectable living as a memory performer. His basic method was to associate numbers with factual information available to him (such as the distance from New York to Harrisburg or the Chinese population of Texas in 1910), thus exemplifying one of the principles of Ericsson's skilled memory theory described later, that of making meaningless material meaningful. Jones found that K's performance on digit span, paired associate learning of words, and a test of logical memory was well below the norm for adults and close to the level of his general intelligence test performance. He concludes (p. 374), "We are not then confronted with the task of explaining a high memory ability coupled with a dull intelligence, but rather with the analysis of the *drive* which has led a person with inferior general capacities ... to devote his life to pseudo-intellectual activity."

Hunter points out that Leslie Welch differed from K in the organised nature of his memory base, which was divided into a number of themes, and that Thomas Macaulay demonstrated, to a greater degree than either K or Welch, the characteristics of absorbed and continuous interactions with a large body of material and organisation of that material. New material was related to the organised database in many ways and thus became available for retrieval in response to many different cues. These cases all illustrate the role of motivation and selective interest in establishing superior memory for material of a certain type, and the variation between individuals in the degree to which such material can be interrelated, organised, and understood. As pointed out earlier, this kind of performance does not in itself demonstrate superior memory ability, as the conditions of acquisition are not controlled. The few controlled tests of K's memory ability suggest it was poor. No such evidence is available in the other two cases. Welch claimed that, when he did not know the answer to a question, if he were given the information he always recalled it the next time the question was asked. General opinion was that this claim was justified. We know nothing, however, of his ability to retain material unrelated to his interests and the same applies to Macaulay.

More thorough early studies of superior memory performance have been reviewed by Ericsson (1985) and Brown and Deffenbacher (1988) and will now be discussed.

Binet (1894) studied three experts on digit recall, two of whom performed mental arithmetic on stage. One of these, Inaudi, also did performances in which he recalled 25 digits presented for a second each and repeated by an assistant, being better with auditory than with visual presentation. He claimed to hear his own voice repeating the input; repeating a vowel during presentation impaired his performance, though it is impossible to tell, as Binet noted, whether this was a general effect of the secondary task or due specifically to its auditory nature. His visual imagery was limited. He could also learn longer lists of digits quickly but his performance on words, prose, and poetry was below average (he had only recently become literate) and his memory for melodies, facts, places, and events in daily life was poor. Inaudi did not describe any special method. He could retain the figures from his previous stage performance

(some 300 digits in all) for up to two days, provided that no other performance intervened.

A second subject, Diamandi, was not very good at recall of auditorily
presented digits. He took three minutes to learn 25 digits presented auditorily, compared with Inaudi's time of 45 seconds. He was, however,
superior to Inaudi when the digits were presented visually. He used a
complex "number form" and claimed that the numbers appeared to him
in his own writing. He may have had some colour synaesthesia for names
of people and days of the week. Binet's third subject, Arnould, was a
mnemonist rather than a calculator and used a system of recoding digits
as consonants, also used by our own subject TE and described later in
the discussion of TE's memory methods. Arnould performed at a similar
level to Diamandi.

Inaudi and Diamandi were primarily expert calculators rather than
mnemonists, so the evidence is derived from a narrow range of tasks and
provides only a modest insight into the basis of their performance. Nevertheless, Binet did a number of studies on their abilities, sufficient to
establish that Inaudi and Diamandi produced differential performance
according to the modality in which the items were presented. Binet also
notes that Inaudi needed to practise regularly to maintain his calculating
ability (which depended heavily on memory), as his performance deterio-
rated during a month when he was otherwise engaged. The most likely
conclusion is that all three subjects depended on very specific methods.

A more interesting subject, studied by both Müller (1911, 1913) and
Hegge (1929), was Dr Rückle of Göttingen. He too specialised in memorisation of numbers and also did calculations in stage performances. He
could repeat back 25 digits read at 1 per second if they were grouped to
form 5 numbers each 5 digits long. For ungrouped lists he needed a
slower rate of presentation to achieve this level; at 1 digit per second he
could retain 18 items, though on one occasion he repeated 60 digits
backwards and forwards when they were read at this rate. He learned a 5
× 5 matrix in 20.2 seconds, reduced to an average of 12.7 seconds when
he was tested again about a year later, compared with 45 seconds for
Inaudi and 180 seconds for Diamandi. In learning longer strings, Rückle
was also superior, followed by Inaudi, Arnould, and Diamandi in that
order. He used his knowledge about features of and associations to
numbers (for example 427 was the birth date of Plato) and also claimed
to experience strong visual imagery. Ericsson (1985) has argued that
Rückle's memory performance cannot have depended on spontaneous
visual imagery, since he took longer to memorise digits and their colours
than to memorise digits alone.

Rückle also showed good memory for nonsense syllables, learning 24
simultaneously presented syllables in an average time of 117.5 seconds in

the original tests and 222.5 seconds in the later tests, compared with Ebbinghaus's time of 400 seconds. In another test he was shown a series of 16 nonsense syllables for less than one second each. The sequence was repeated four times, then 9½ minutes later he was given a recognition test in which they were mixed with eight foils; no information is given on how the interval was occupied. Rückle's average probability of a hit was 0.92 and his false alarm probability was only 0.04. A control group produced a hit probability of 0.38 (no false alarm rate is given). Hegge presented Rückle with 100 concrete nouns for about 10 seconds each and he recalled 71 of them. However, there is no certainty that this was an exceptional level of performance; another subject studied by the same experimenter scored 95% correct, using the method of loci. Rückle said that he had no special methods to cope with words and was confused by the images they aroused. This problem was also experienced by Luria's subject S described later. At first sight this observation appears to conflict with the evidence described earlier that Rückle had no special ability to retain coloured images of words, but careful consideration can resolve this apparent conflict. In the case of the words Rückle is claiming that images for the *associations* to the words were readily evoked from memory. In attempting to memorise words and colours, it was his ability to process both in parallel, rather than the strength of any images associated with the words, that was tested. Inability to carry out such parallel processing does not preclude the possibility that Rückle possessed particularly rich and strong visual associations to words developed during normal day-to-day exposure.

Müller retested Rückle about a year after his original experiments, giving him numbers and other material. His performance on numbers had improved. Mean time to learn 25 digits had decreased from 20.2 to 12.7 seconds and in a later test (Müller, 1913) time per item for 102 digits was 1.7 seconds and for 204 digits it was 2.5 seconds. However, time to learn non-numerical material had increased. As indicated earlier, mean time to learn 24 nonsense syllables went up from 117.5 to 222.5 seconds. Other tests used were learning 12 colour names (an increase from 30 to 33.5 seconds on average) and 20 consonants (an increase from 43.5 to 69 seconds). Without control data we do not know if these times were superior to normal subjects.

Müller explains the improvement on numbers by pointing out that Rückle had spent the year in mathematical studies, especially in reducing large numbers to their prime factors, and had thereby established an extensive knowledge of the properties of numbers. He employed this knowledge to aid retention, in preference to factual information such as Plato's birth date, which he had used previously. It is not clear why this led to impairment on the other materials.

Rückle's ability was less restricted than that of Binet's subjects. It is clear that his numerical memory depended heavily on associations to numbers and knowledge about their properties. In his first investigation, Müller (1911) gives a detailed account of how Rückle structured long numbers. Groups of six digits (Komplexe) were divided into two Teilcomplexe, each of three digits. These were reduced to products of two prime numbers, if possible in a form providing easy associations: 893047 became $19 \times 47 = 893$, $1 \times 47 = 047$. Long sequences were stored by associations between Komplexe or by position tags. Manipulation of recall conditions, such as asking for recall in groups of five, confirmed this analysis.

Müller (1913) says that Rückle murmured numbers to himself while learning, combining them into groups of 6, 3, or 4, according to the task constraints, and naming these groups. It seems that his use of his numerical knowledge enabled an already unusually good memory, as evidenced by his performance with some other types of material, to produce exceptional performance with numbers. He was clearly also a man of exceptional intelligence.

A Japanese researcher, Susukita (1933, 1934), studied Ishihara, who gave stage performances and once memorised 2400 digits in four hours with 99.7% accuracy, using a method of converting them into syllables. (In the 1993 World Memory Championships Dominic O'Brien memorised 900 digits perfectly in one hour.) Ishihara specialised in learning long series of numbers, though he also demonstrated excellent ability with names, consonants, nonsense syllables, and shapes. Susukita's first report concentrates on memorisation of numbers in order to compare his findings with the results from Diamandi, Arnould, and Rückle, no comparable data being available for other types of material. Susukita's second report compares Ishihara with three Japanese control subjects in learning both numerical and other types of list.

In the standard experimental procedure, random sequences of numbers were presented in rows and learning time was measured from exposure to Ishihara's signal that he was ready to recall them. Recall was normally in the original order, but Ishihara could recall backwards if requested or give separate rows. Susukita presents total time until completion of written recall of lists up to 200 items in length, for Diamandi, Arnould, and Ishihara (separate times for learning alone were not available in the case of the first two subjects). The results, converted to time per item, are given in Fig. 2.1 and demonstrate that Ishihara was far superior to Binet's two subjects. Separate learning and recall times were available for Rückle and Fig. 2.2 gives learning time per item over the lower range for both Ishihara and Rückle (errors were minimal for both subjects over this range). Susukita includes data

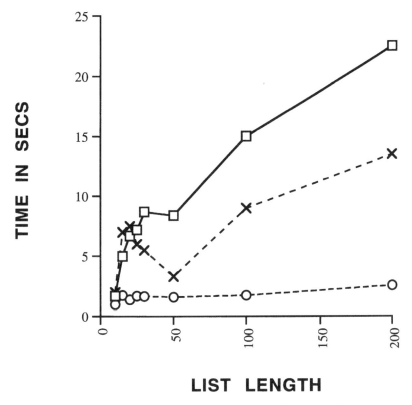

Fig. 2.1. Mean time per item in seconds to learn and recall lists up to 200 items in length for three mnemonists (squares = Arnould; crosses = Diamandi; circles = Ishihara).

from Inaudi in his second paper, who demonstrated a much slower acquisition rate than either Rückle or Ishihara. The results again demonstrate the high quality of Ishihara's performance compared with other experts.

Susukita also presents more detailed figures for separate learning and recall times for Ishihara. Up to 200 items, recall time remained constant at about one second per item, so the increases in Fig. 2.1 as load increases are due to learning time per item rather than recall time. Errors were virtually non-existent up to a list length of 200 but, with lists of more than 200 items, a steady increase in errors is apparent and recall times became quite variable between trials (data from two trials are reported up to a list length of 1200 items, which both yield fairly similar learning times, but for lists of length 1800, 2400, and 2502 only one trial was given). The last of these was learned earlier than the second and, though learning time was shorter, errors were far more

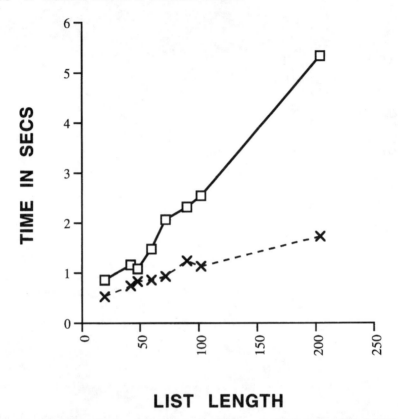

Fig. 2.2.   Mean time per item in seconds to learn lists up to 204 items in length for Rückle (squares) and Ishihara (crosses). Figures for Rückle are from tasks given in 1911–1912.

frequent. Table 2.1 gives Ishihara's mean times per item and error probability for lists of more than 200 items.

Ishihara had two basic mnemonic aids, foundations (Grundlage) and complexes (Teilkomplexe). Foundations were representations of places, of which he had a stock of over 400. Complexes were formed from Japanese kana symbols for digits, which were then combined to form words for multidigit numbers. Japanese lends itself readily to such a method. Each digit was represented by several possible kana symbols. The numeral 1 (ichi) could be represented by ichi, i, hi, bi, pi; the numeral 2 (ni) by ni, fu, bu, pu, zi. Hence, 12 could be hizi, meaning elbow, which was pictured as a naked elbow. Such a complex would then be associated with one of the locations represented in a foundation. It is not stated whether the foundations consisted of a series of locations in a fixed order, as in the classical method of loci (only one example is given). However, this seems highly probable as it is unclear how a series of such founda-

TABLE 2.1
Ishihara's Mean Learning Time Per Item and Error Probability in Learning Lists of
More Than 200 Items

	No. of items							
	204	300	600	900	1200	1800	2400	2502[1]
t (secs)	1.7	2.0	3.6	4.3	4.6	4.5	6.2	5.3
p	0.01	0.01	0.01	0.01	0.02	0.02	0.02	0.11

[1]This list was learned before the list of 2400 items.

tions could be organised otherwise in order to maintain the order of the numbers. With longer lists of over 300 lines of digits (six digits per line), two or three complexes would be linked to each foundation.

The full method is illustrated in the following example, shown in Table 2.2, of how Ishihara learned the number sequence

7 4 2 7 6 9 1 1 3 8

9 0 9 2 5 1 0 3 4 6.

These methods, as well as enabling the rapid learning already demonstrated, also produced substantial retention over a month, as shown in Fig. 2.3.

In his second article Susukita discusses Ishihara's learning of names and nonsense syllables and demonstrates his enormous superiority over three control subjects. To learn 10 male names the control subjects took an overall average time of almost six minutes, while Ishihara took 43 seconds on average.

Detailed investigations yielded no evidence for eidetic imagery. Though Susukita presents no explicit discussion of Ishihara's methods with non-numerical material, he implies that basically the same techniques were employed. Two main sources of errors with numbers are noted, one where abstract words created difficulty in finding a suitable representation and another when the complex representing the word was not easily fitted into the foundation. For example, when 136 was represented as "isamu" (to be brave), Ishihara could only associate this with a vague feeling and later pointed out that if he had used "hizaro" (meaning "sitting with crossed legs") he could have placed himself in front of a man sitting by the fire with crossed legs. The second type of error is illustrated by a failure to recall the number 163, which he had associated with "hirosa" (white or bright), but he had difficulty linking this to his foundation, which was "room". He said that the connection

TABLE 2.2
Ishihara's Method of Learning a Particular Number Sequence

Step	Foundation	Number Sequence	Interpretation	Complex Representation
1	a field by his house at home	74	nashi—pear	a pear tree in a field by his house
2	a brook flowing between his house and the field	27	funa—carp	carp swimming in the brook by his house
3	a high building on his home estate	69	mugi—wheat	a heap of wheat in front of the building
4	the rice field at his house	1138	ii muja— a splendid Shinto temple	a beautiful Shinto temple in the rice field
5	a relative's house	90	kum—bear	a bear in a cage by the relative's house
6	a friend's house	925	kuniya— country (or national flag)	a child waving the national flag in front of the friend's house
7	acquaintance's house	103	hitomi—pupil (of the eye)	a beautiful girl with bright eyes standing by the house
8	a house with a white wall (which is rare), near his home	46	shiro—white	the white wall of this house

would have been easier if the foundation had been something evoking brightness, like a field.

It is clear from these detailed accounts that Ishihara relied on a method of recoding the numbers into meaningful words, then associating images of the objects denoted by these words with other associates in order to retain the sequence. It is unclear whether these other associates (the foundations) were organised in a fixed order or linked by fresh associations each time. The former would seem to be more likely, as retention of the sequence could not be highly reliable in the latter case. Clearly Ishihara

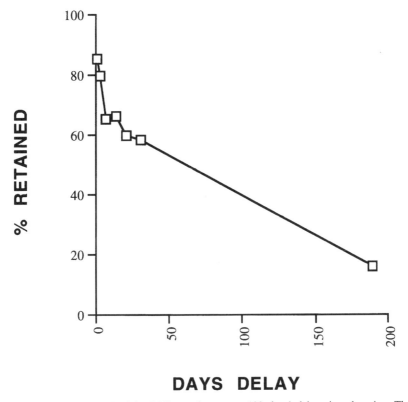

Fig. 2.3. Percentage retained by Ishihara after up to 189 days' delay since learning. The retention figure for 189 days is from Susukita (1934, Fig. 3) and the other figures are from Susukita (1933, Table 10).

possessed strong motivation and persistence in developing and practising these methods. No evidence is given on whether or not he possessed unusual memory ability without his method, since no tasks were given to which his method could not be applied and he was not questioned about his early ability or the abilities of his relatives.

Finkelstein (Bousfield & Barry, 1933; Sandor, 1932; Weinland, 1948) also demonstrated exceptional ability for calculation and memorisation of numbers. His letter span was average and his memory for visual forms somewhat below average, according to Sandor, though no evidence is given. Finkelstein did not discover his talent until he was 22 years old and there is no mention of any relative with similar talent. He believed himself to be a genius, but he showed no talent other than one for routine calculation, and the general consensus is that his other talents were modest. There is, however, no convincing evidence for Sandor's claim that his reasoning ability was impaired due to his fixation with memorising.

Finkelstein claimed to see spoken numbers written in his own handwriting and believed this to be a form of eidetic imagery (unjustifiably). However, no standard measurement of digit span for auditorily presented material is available, because he claimed he could memorise numbers indefinitely if they were presented at one per second but refused to be tested on this task. Weinland does describe Finkelstein's repetition of a visually presented 17-digit number backwards "immediately", giving some support to Finkelstein's claim of vivid imagery, but the speed of recall is not reported. Weinland gives detailed records of his recall of digit strings presented visually and very rapidly, which demonstrate exceptional speed of perceptual encoding as well as unusual memory. These tests show that he was able to repeat back a visual sequence of 39 items displayed for only four seconds and one of 30 items displayed for three or four seconds. In some earlier experiments at Ohio State University reported in *Popular Science Monthly* (September, 1936), he learned a 21-digit number in 4.43 seconds, while another subject HW, after 75 hours' training, matched this feat in 4.37 seconds. Clearly Finkelstein's performance had improved by the time Weinland reported on him in 1948. This and the feat of HW indicate the role of practice.

Sandor provides data on Finkelstein's speed of learning number strings of different lengths, which show that his performance was similar to that of Inaudi, but inferior to Rückle. Weinland also shows that Finkelstein took about 18 seconds to learn a 5 × 5 number matrix (later reduced to 9 seconds according to one report) and 5 minutes 44 seconds to learn a 4 × 17 number matrix (though two numbers were recalled erroneously in the latter case). Using a 6 × 8 matrix with several memory experts employing mnemonic techniques we have obtained perfect recall after study times ranging from 72 to 721 seconds, with a mean of 342 seconds, suggesting Finkelstein's performance was extremely good. No data are available on Finkelstein's delayed recall, as he refused to be tested, claiming that his performance would be perfect if he knew such a test was intended.

The main basis of Finkelstein's performance was undoubtedly practice and a rich fund of associations to numbers (dates, telephone numbers, squares, square roots, and other properties), usually to three- or four-digit sequences. No evidence emerges for any natural memory ability or ability in any other field than number memorisation. His speed of encoding numbers seems to have been unusually rapid, but no tests are reported using non-numerical material.

Apart from Rückle and Ishihara, none of these cases yields convincing evidence for superior performance dependent on anything other than techniques devised to encode strings of digits. Though few of the tests given to these subjects involved material other than numbers, it seems likely that these performers, if they had possessed some more general ability, would have either demonstrated it in public performances or been tested by the investigator. Hence the absence of data is unlikely to be simply the result of cursory test procedures. Even Rückle and Ishihara do not appear to have demonstrated conclusively any abilities other than practised methods of recoding numerical material. The claims of several of these subjects to possess especially vivid imagery are not supported by any experimental data other than in the case of Rückle, where the results fail to confirm his claim conclusively.

The concentration on numerical tests does have the advantage of enabling some comparison of the abilities of the different subjects to be undertaken; though methods were rarely exactly the same, they were sufficiently similar to make such comparisons reasonably informative. We will wait until later when other subjects can be included, before attempting to derive any conclusions from such comparisons.

LATER STUDIES

More detailed case studies of individual subjects have been reported over the last 20 years, involving tests on a much wider range of material. These permit a review of the nature of memory rather than simply enabling individuals to be compared for the power of their memory on one type of task. However, since the selection of tasks is quite varied, it is difficult to compare the different individuals adequately with a view to establishing similarities and differences in the patterns of their abilities.

Luria (1975) recorded his extended study of Shereshevskii; Hunter (1962, 1977) described the abilities of Aitken; and Hunt and Love (1972) reported their systematic tests of VP, which served as a model for the study of TE by Gordon, Valentine, and Wilding (1984). Ericsson and his co-workers (e.g. Ericsson, 1985; Ericsson & Polson, 1988a) have reported acquisition of remarkable digit spans by two subjects and memory for dinner orders in a waiter. Thompson, Cowan, Frieman, Mahadevan, Vogl, and Frieman (1991) and Biederman, Cooper, Mahadevan, and Fox (1992) have reported on the memory abilities of Rajan Mahadevan and Thompson, Cowan, and Frieman (1993) provide more detailed data, including tests of Rajan's ability to retrieve digit sequences from the first 10,000 places of pi. Ceci, deSimone, and Johnson (1992) describe the memory of Bubbles P. A few studies have reported specific abilities in subjects whose memory ability was otherwise normal (Gummerman & Gray, 1971, on retention of visual pictures; Coltheart & Glick, 1974, on backward spelling; Novoa, Fein, & Obler, 1988, on language learning).

Others have described unusual memory ability for a particular type of material in autistic subjects, combined with poor performance on other cognitive tasks (Obler & Fein, 1988). The rest of this chapter will provide a detailed description and assessment of these studies.

Luria's Study of S

Luria's study was first published in English in 1968[1]. His description of the memory abilities of Shereshevskii (S) is a classic of research on superior memory. Luria first met S in the late 1920s when S was just under 30 years old, but the earliest of the observations recorded in Luria's account dates from December 1932 and the majority are from the mid-1930s. S was referred to Luria by the editor of the newspaper for whom he worked as a reporter. His editor had discovered that S had verbatim recall, without taking notes, for the oral instructions issued to reporters at the beginning of the day. Luria set out to test the limitations of S's memory and came to the conclusion (p. 32) that his memory was "virtually unlimited". Luria believed (p. 52), and his view has subsequently been widely accepted, that "There is no question that S's exceptional memory was an innate characteristic and that the techniques he used were merely superimposed on an existing structure and did not 'stimulate' it with devices other than those which were natural to it." However, the interpretation of S's ability remains uncertain and Luria's conclusion has been questioned by Ericsson and Chase (1982), who focus their scepticism on S's claim that he retained a photograph-like image of a number matrix. Luria supports this claim by reporting confusions of numbers of similar appearance such as 3 and 8 (p. 23). However, a subject who recalls by "reading" a matrix would show little difference in speed between recalling rows and columns or between recalling left-to-right and in the reverse order (some slight bias might be expected in favour of the normal direction of reading). Like several other subjects tested on this task (Ericsson & Chase, 1982; Wilding & Valentine, 1985, 1994a), S took longer in recalling columns than rows and generally longer on backwards than on forwards recall, suggesting that the material was stored in a form which required some transformation in order to meet the recall requirements. Several of the other subjects tested on this task, who showed a similar pattern of recall speed to that of S, described methods which clearly did not involve visual images, but which did require additional operations to produce recall by columns or in reverse order. It is also significant that S seems to have shown no superiority in recalling visual over acoustic material. We agree with Ericsson and Chase's scepticism concerning Luria's belief that S retained a visual image of the matrix.

---

[1] All references here are to the 1975 Penguin edition.

Ericsson and Chase (p. 611) go on to argue that data from the matrix learning task "are the only objective evidence supporting Luria's claim that S had a structurally unique memory. The rest of S's memory is based on standard mnemonic techniques". However, this wider scepticism is less convincing. Admittedly, Luria rarely provides numerical records defining S's performance, but his recorded observations over a period of many years (see later for examples) suggest that Ericsson and Chase are oversimplifying the case. It is also true that most of the evidence consists of a record of S's description of his mental experiences when attempting recall and Luria accepted these at face value rather than attempting to devise tests to provide supporting evidence. However, S's memory performance is in many cases difficult to explain simply in terms of mnemonic methods.

Furthermore, Luria describes how S developed the main methods he used as a method of keeping his unusual spontaneous mental processes under control (p. 36) and improving his stage performance, rather than simply to increase the quantity of material he could retain. Unfortunately it is not clear from Luria's account of his first meeting with S to what extent some mnemonic methods were already an important element in his abilities. On the one hand S claimed to be unaware that there was anything unusual about his memory, but on the other hand Luria does not definitely deny that he was already using the method of loci, which he refined later as a major technique in his repertoire. Luria first met S in the 1920s (p. 16), but the first account of S using the method of loci is from 1932 (p. 33), where he explains how he overlooked an object that merged into the background where it was placed, and the improvements seem to have been devised in about 1935 (p. 36ff.). However, Luria reports that at the first meeting S required words to be read slowly and distinctly (p. 17), with a three- to four-second pause between each item (p. 18), and later points out that the reason for this was to prevent images coalescing into each other (p. 31). This comment is in the context of a discussion of locating images in some geographical sequence, so the implication is that S was indeed using the method of loci, perhaps in a relatively unsophisticated way, even at their first meeting. Luria also notes that S could recall in reverse order as well as in forward order (p. 18), a feat which he later ascribes to use of the method of loci (p. 31). Nevertheless, Luria believed that S's spontaneous imagery was the key feature of his unusual memory and later describes (p. 86ff.) how S rapidly became confused when listening to a story because of multiple spontaneous images, and had difficulty focusing on the meaning. This account, however, is not completely consistent with S's ability to recall his editor's instructions perfectly, which resulted in him being referred to Luria in the first place. Thus we are left in some doubt about the important characteristics of S's memory at this first meeting with Luria.

Despite these uncertainties, we can attempt to derive an overall picture of the major features of S's memory and to determine in what respects (if any) it was unusual. There seems to be little doubt that from an early age S experienced strong spontaneous synaesthesia, particularly to sounds, which evoked smudges, splashes, and taste sensations, that were consistent on different occasions. He once referred to Vygotsky's "crumbly, yellow voice" and individual numbers and letters had their own colour and shape associations (pp. 26–27). S claimed that these occurred from a very early age (p. 24); "It was only later, after his facility for logical and figurative memory had developed, that these tended to fade into the background, though they continued to play some part in his recall" (p. 28). Luria implies, but did not carry out any specific tests of this, that synaesthetic impressions were often the source of S's memory ability (e.g. p. 51). Another characteristic was the rapid evocation of spontaneous associations, for example to the elements of the meaningless formula described in Chapter 1, which were predominantly visual and seem to have occurred in an uncontrolled manner ("I found myself on Pushkin Square", p. 36; or see the account of S's associations to stories, p. 88). These images were evoked by familiar words (unfamiliar words evoked line patterns, p. 30) and were additional to the synaesthetic experiences, which they could overwrite. The images were consistent from occasion to occasion, this being the basis for long-term recall, together with the synaesthetic experiences. While such associations may have been a consequence of S's practice of mnemonic methods, Luria's account indicates that S had to learn to control them rather than learn to produce them.

The associations evoked by words were frequently (perhaps always) particular sounds and images rather than general aspects of meaning. Thus, S could not appreciate that different words could refer to the same object (p. 75), that one word could have different meanings indicated by context (p. 91) (though he seems to have employed the word "zhuk" for a multitude of referents), that objects can be grouped into semantic categories (p. 49), or that words could be interpreted metaphorically (p. 91). S interpreted elements of a story literally (usually as a visual image), and therefore had problems in integrating it into a whole, whenever minor variations in words or descriptions occurred. (He also had a similar problem in recognising the same face with different expressions, p. 53). Abstract words completely baffled him (p. 100) and reading and understanding poetry was "a nightmare" (p.93). These observations suggest that S did not build up a propositional structure or imagine an action sequence from the prose he heard but only derived images and arbitrary associations to the input. His coding was predominantly surface, concrete, and particular rather than deep, abstract, and general. Presumably, though, he was able to act on the series of instructions he received from his newspaper editor; it would be interesting to know whether he organised them into a plan or merely retained them in sequence and retrieved them one by one from his perfect memory. It seems unlikely that the problems described were purely a result of his learning of mnemonic methods. Rather, it seems that processes, similar to those which produced random visual smudges and lines to meaningless sounds, evoked more complex visual images to words, once he had learned their meaning. It is the unusual nature of S's encoding processes which affected his memory rather than the reverse, producing a much more literal record than in the normal person. Normally, the brain abstracts and retains meaning, rather than the surface features of the input.

Synaesthesia has been experienced by a number of people in the arts world, including the poet Rimbaud, the writer Nabokov, and the composer Messiaen. Reichard, Jakobson, and Werth (1949) give an anecdotal account of this phenomenon. Baron-Cohen and his colleagues have in the last few years studied one type of synaesthesia more systematically (Baron-Cohen, Harrison, Goldstein, & Wyke, 1993; Baron-Cohen, Wyke, & Binnie, 1987;). When seeking volunteers for their study they found a huge preponderance of women claiming synaesthetic experiences (210 women wrote in compared with only 2 men) and when their subjects reported that a relative also had the condition, the relative was invariably a woman. This suggests a sex-linked genetic basis. For this reason alone, it is clear that S was unusual. Comparison of the reports suggests that his synaesthesia also differed considerably from the type studied by Baron-Cohen and his colleagues. They selected for their second study nine subjects reporting colour sensations to speech and found that it was the initial letter of words which determined the reported colour (though the single subject studied in the original paper had experienced colours to words as wholes). The colours reported were highly consistent over a year and several letters evoked the same colour across most of the subjects. Reichard et al. (1949) indicate that synaesthesia can sometimes be used to aid memory and the subject of Baron-Cohen et al.'s (1987) study reported that the synaesthesia aided memory such as that for a person's name, though this could cause a problem when two different names evoked the same colour. There is no indication in the second study of any more pervasive relation between synaesthesia and memory ability. None of the subjects apparently possessed superior memory ability or gave any indication that synaesthesia was an important factor in memory. There is no discussion on whether they had any problem with abstract thought of the type S experienced, but since they were recruited through a radio science discussion programme this does not seem highly likely.

S's synaesthesia, on the other hand, was not confined to colours or even to visual sensations, but was much stronger and richer than that of these subjects, producing a qualitative change in his style of thought. Every speech sound had "its own distinct form, colour and taste" (p. 26). Luria claims (p. 28) that the synaesthetic experiences aided recall by "furnishing him with additional 'extra' information that would guarantee accurate recall. If ... S was prompted to reproduce a word inaccurately, the additional synaesthetic sensations he experienced would fail to coincide with the word he produced, leaving him with the sense that something was wrong". Presumably it was for this reason that he had a problem in understanding the identical reference of near synonyms when reading prose (mentioned earlier).

Baron-Cohen et al. suggest that synaesthesia may result from inadequate separation of modular systems in the cerebral cortex handling different types of input, due to abnormal brain development or inadequate mutual inhibition. Cytowic (1989; see also Cytowic & Wood, 1982, for an earlier review of theories) believes that the critical sites are in the limbic system, but agrees on the general nature of the abnormality. Both sides have cited evidence of abnormal brain activity, revealed by scanning methods, in the areas critical for their theory. In many subjects, including those tested by Baron-Cohen and his colleagues, only one set of connections appears to have been involved but in S the abnormalities appear to have been more widespread. One of our own subjects, described later, also showed indications of synaesthesia more like that displayed by S than by Baron-Cohen's subjects.

A further argument for the unusual nature of S's memory is his ability to retain without intent, not only material deliberately learned such as the formula given earlier, but also incidental visual images of the test situation (p. 19): "You were sitting at the table and I in the rocking chair ... You were wearing a grey suit and you looked at me like this." The sceptic can of course argue that no check of the accuracy of such incidental observations is possible, nor do we have control data demonstrating what a normal subject can accomplish. What is clear is that S could recall after many years enormous quantities of arbitrary material. Luria (p. 19) claims that such recall was invariably successful. Indeed S's problem was in forgetting unwanted material rather than in retention.

Though he carried out no systematic investigation, Luria commented that some of S's relatives may have shown similar tendencies to superior memory ability, but the evidence provided is completely indecisive (p. 52). There is a fascinating description of S's earliest memory (p. 61), which he suggests may date from his first year of life (unusually early). As is common in such cases, it is impossible to verify this claim, but the nature of the description is such as to suggest a very primitive understanding of the situation described and is therefore consistent with the claim.

The profile of S bears a marked resemblance to more extreme examples of unusual memory that are found in some cases of autism or Asperger's syndrome (e.g. Kanner, 1943; Rimland, 1964; see also cases discussed later in this chapter). Remarkable memory for literal information, such as positions of objects, routes, music, etc., can be combined with severely impaired ability to interpret meaning, social conventions, and "other minds" (Baron-Cohen, Leslie, & Frith, 1985). Some additional evidence will be provided below that a similar pattern can occur in some mnemonic experts who do not show the full autistic profile.

It is therefore argued here that S possessed an abnormal system for encoding input from the senses, which produced rich and ramifying associations, but he failed to abstract the "deeper" levels of meaning, such as categorisation and symbolic meanings. This resulted in unusual ability to retain surface characteristics, but also impaired understanding.

In response to the questions posed in Chapter 1, we would conclude that S probably demonstrated superior memory of a general rather than specific nature (though the data on which this conclusion rests are somewhat limited), that he employed techniques but these are not the complete explanation for his achievements, that his memory was qualitatively different from and not just quantitatively superior to normal human memory, that his memory was unusual at an early age; and that other members of the family may also have had unusual memories (Luria, p. 52). His imagery was obviously exceptionally strong, but his ability for abstract thought limited.

Hunt and Love's Study of VP

In 1972 Hunt and Love published a much more analytic study than Luria's on the memory of a man known as VP, which represented at that time the only other account of a memory ability to match that of S. They tested VP on a wide variety of memory tasks (the Atkinson–Shiffrin keeping track task, described below in the section on TE's memory, story recall, a test of eidetic imagery which demonstrated that he possessed no such ability, memory for number matrices, chess positions, nominal phrases, visual digit span, the Sternberg memory search task, the Brown–Peterson test of short-term memory, and memory for line drawings of objects). On nearly all of these his performance was far superior to that of the control groups. Unfortunately they did not systematically question VP on his methods (if any) for tackling each task. However, it is clear that VP presented a very different profile from that of S in many respects. He showed no trace of synaesthesia or vivid visual imagery. Indeed his spatial and visualisation abilities seem to have been rather modest (pp. 239, 240, 243–244, 254), though this is somewhat at odds with the claim that he knew the street map of Riga at the age of five years. His performance when memorising numbers depended on searching for a meaningful association such as a date, then recalling what he was doing on the day in question. With nonsense syllables he drew on his knowledge of many European languages to find a meaningful associate.

It would, however, be a gross oversimplification to conclude that VP's ability depended solely on skill in finding meaningful associations to meaningless material. He also performed at a very high level on a number of tasks where an explicit recoding method was not appropriate. On Sternberg's short-term memory scanning task his speed of response was unaffected by the length of list in memory, suggesting he was able to scan the list in parallel. At the age of 10 he memorised 150 poems for a competition. He was given Bartlett's "War of the Ghosts" story to read through twice and then recalled it immediately and six weeks later. The authors used as a measure the number of nouns and verbs he recalled. This rather crude measure yielded 62% at immediate recall and 59% six weeks later, compared with 45% and 32% recalled by a control group. The measure requires exact recall rather than gist, which might include synonyms and paraphrases, so should not be compared with the number of story elements recalled, which we used in our own studies of story recall reported later. VP showed superior recall and very superior retention.

He believed that his ability was largely the result of schooling, which required a large amount of rote memorisation, combined with a "passive attitude", which both caused him to accept this regime and also to develop a general cognitive style of absorbing information rather than operating on it to achieve wider goals. Though this claim has some superficial resemblance to our earlier categorisation of S as a "surface processor" who did not abstract meaning, VP was not a surface processor in this sense. He had no problem in understanding the meaning of prose passages, he coded chess positions according to the function rather than the visual pattern of the pieces, and he organised pictures according to semantic rather than visual similarities. It seems rather that it was the further steps of organising or reorganising information in new ways that were missing, especially in view of his measured IQ of 136 on the WAIS.

VP showed superior performance over a wide range of tasks. It is not possible to decide conclusively on the basis of the account given whether early training was indeed the key factor in developing his memory ability. He claimed that other children who had experienced a similar regime were able to memorise as well as he could or even better than him. Hunt and Love do not describe his schooling experience before the age of 10, so we do not know whether his early schooling required extensive use of memory. (Since he came from a Jewish tradition that stressed rote learning, the presumption is that it did.) After that age he attended a school with very few books, which required him to rely heavily on memory. Prior to attending school, however, he is said to have begun to read at the age of 3½ and to have memorised rail and bus timetables and the map of Riga (a city of about half a million people) by the age of 5, though it is not clear exactly what this last claim entailed. These facts all suggest unusual early ability, contrary to his own belief that his skill was entirely learned. No information is given on whether any of his relatives possessed unusual memory ability.

Professor Aitken

Hunter (1977) describes the memory abilities of Aitken, Professor of Mathematics at Edinburgh University, having previously described his mathematical abilities (Hunter, 1962). Hunter's account is largely anecdotal, but does include some limited data on digit span performance and on long-term retention of digit and word lists. When tested in 1932, Aitken achieved an auditory letter span of 10, an auditory digit span of 13, and a visual digit span of 15. His auditory digit span reached a maximum of 15 in 1960 when the digits were read to him in groups of 5, presented at a rate of 5 digits per second, with a one-second pause between groups. He used rhythm to group the items and his knowledge of mathematics in allowing associations to emerge spontaneously to groups of numbers. Hence, while meaningful recoding was clearly taking place, Aitken made no deliberate use of mnemonics, for which he had a marked distaste. The method seems not dissimilar to that of VP, but automatic rather than deliberate, and based on knowledge of the proper-ties of numbers rather than other types of association to them. He stressed the importance of relaxing to "let the properties of the material reveal themselves" and, if long-term retention was required, of allowing material to "soak in". When he learned pi to 1000 places (a modest feat compared with those of Rajan and others discussed later) he reported that learning groups of 50 arranged in 10 subgroups of 5 was easy when a rhythm and tempo was established.

However, Aitken's ability was not restricted to memorising numbers. He was said to have been able to memorise the names and initials of a new class list of 35 pupils after a single reading and to have been able to recite books of Virgil and Milton's *Paradise Lost* in his youth. More objective evidence is also available. He learned a list of 25 words, after hearing them four times at one item per second. This feat itself was not spectacular, but he could remember the list correctly 28 years later! No special coding method for this feat is implied in Hunter's account. The comments on his recall show that he used structure derived from rhythmic grouping. Aitken's recall of the names and numbers of an entire platoon of 39 men has also been recounted in Chapter 1. However, he retained rather less of a list of 16 three-digit numbers, which he learned during six presentations. Four years later he produced 12 correct groups and 28 years later he recalled 9, though in neither case were these in the correct order. Recently Hunter (1996) has provided new evidence on Aitken's recall of a version of Bartlett's "War of the Ghosts" (Bartlett, 1932), 26 years after he first read it twice in 1934. We compared the original version with Aitken's recall, using the same measure as that employed by Hunt and Love (1972) when testing VP (the number of nouns and verbs recalled). This revealed that Aitken recalled 58% of the original, as much as VP after six weeks and more than control subjects at immediate recall! In combination, these rather fragmentary data suggest an exceptional ability to retain incidentally encountered or deliberately learned verbal information, as well as unusual facility in organising and retaining numerical information. No evidence is given on Aitken's childhood abilities, his imagery ability, or the abilities of other members of his family. He was obviously highly intelligent.

TE

The memory ability of TE was described by Gordon et al. (1984) and Wilding and Valentine (1985). The first of these studies employed several of the tasks employed by Hunt and Love in their study of VP (the Atkinson–Shiffrin keeping track task, number matrices, recall of nominal phrases, the Brown–Peterson short-term memory task, and visual digit span). The second study employed three tasks with somewhat greater ecological validity: recall of a story, face recognition, and recall of names to faces. These tasks are described in detail in Chapter 4.

TE was a philosophy student at the time of the original testing (he went on to take a first-class degree). He did stage performances involving conjuring and memory feats, which relied on a number of methods he had developed since the age of 15 (see later). The Atkinson–Shiffrin keeping track task (Fig. 2.4) presents one of four possible nonsense syllables on each trial, each paired with a two-digit number, which changes on each trial. On test trials a nonsense syllable alone is presented and recall of the last number paired with it is required. Success rate can be plotted against lag since the last appearance of the syllable being tested. Over 140 test trials, testing lags up to 22 items in length, TE made only 3 errors. These were all in fact due to a single error in recalling the

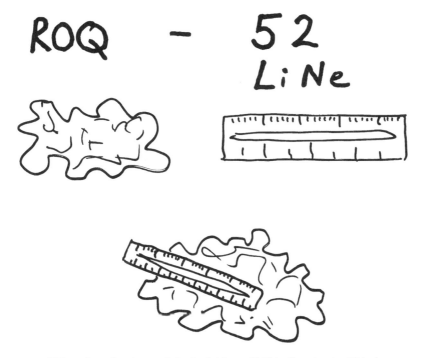

Fig. 2.4.   TE's coding of an item pair in the Atkinson–Shiffrin "keeping track" task.

last number associated with the syllable DEF. Instead of the correct answer, which was 39, TE recalled the last number associated with CUH, which was 34. He then added the next number, 13, to CUH instead of DEF. Hence, the next time he recalled numbers to both these syllables, he was incorrect. VP made no errors on this task. On the visual digit span task items were presented at one per second. TE achieved an average span over five test runs of 12.2 items, with a maximum of 15 items.

A major component in his skill was the use of the figure alphabet (Table 2.3, also used by Arnould, as mentioned earlier), whereby each digit is associated with one or more letters, organised in phonemically similar clusters (e.g. 1 can be T, D, or Th, 2 is N or Ng, 3 is M, etc. Several of these pairings make use of approximate visual similarity of the letter and digit to aid learning). Number sequences can then be converted to words by inserting vowels in the derived consonant sequence. Hence, 164 might become TeaCHeR. TE also used additional methods to help retain such encoding and especially to aid in the retention of the order of longer sequences. Visual images played a major part. The sequence 164359 became TeaCHeR MaiLBox, recalled as a teacher posting a letter into a mailbox (or even a teacher being posted into a mailbox!). To

TABLE 2.3
The Figure Alphabet

Digit	Letter	Other Characters
1	T	TH
2	N	Ng
3	M	
4	R	
5	L	
6	J	G(soft) Ch Sh
7	K	G(soft) Q C(hard)
8	F	V
9	P	B
0	Z	S C(soft)

maintain the information that this was the first line of numbers in a matrix, TE used a set of prelearned picture associations to numbers : 1—eat, 2—inn, 3—aim, etc. For the first row, "eat" evoked a canteen and therefore the sequence of events linking "teacher" and "mailbox" was visualised in a canteen. Since the canteen was linked only to "teacher" and "teacher" only to "mailbox", the correct sequence of the latter two elements was preserved unequivocally.

Thus a few simple pre-learned associations and practice in creating images to represent associated objects were combined to handle a variety of tasks. TE was sure that this constituted a full explanation for his performance and claimed that if he did not deploy his techniques his memory was quite unexceptional, for example in an eyewitness situation. However, he also showed exceptional ability (better than any other subject we have tested and better than the best subjects in the original study by Dube, 1977) in recalling a story lasting six minutes on tape, which gave him little scope to use his methods. He recalled 66% of the propositional content immediately and 64% eight days later. He gave one example of using his method in this task, imagining a pond to aid in recalling the word "pondered", but ironically he attributed this to the wrong character when recalling the story and misplaced it in the story sequence! (Further examples will be cited from other mnemonists of inappropriate use of mnemonics distracting from the processing of semantic structure.) He also showed an exceptionally high score (4.8 standard deviations above the mean) on the imaginal thinking scale of the Individual Differences Questionnaire (Paivio & Harshman, 1983); his verbal thinking score was within the normal range. Details of TE's scores are given in Table 4.5 (p. 102), where they can be compared with those of other subjects.

These observations might be explained in terms of development of more general abilities through practice of mnemonic methods or in terms of some pre-existing superiority in memory ability. We have no clear evidence to decide between these two possibilities and think it likely that both are relevant. Though it has been claimed that mnemonic methods do not generalise across tasks, largely on the basis of the finding (e.g. Ericsson & Faivre, 1988) that SF's skill with digits did not result in any improvement in letter span, TE did of course show great skill in adapting his basic methods to handle a number of very different tasks, and indeed in memorising the story apparently without any special methods. Also, some practitioners of mnemonic methods have told us that their general memory ability has improved as a result of practising their methods, though no formal evidence seems to be available on this point. TE claimed that his early memory ability was quite normal until he started practising his methods and made no reference to any other member of his family having superior memory ability. It is also impossible to determine whether his exceptional imagery ability had been developed by practice. He was clearly of a high intelligence level.

Ericsson's Subjects SF, DD, and JC

Ericsson, Chase, and Falloon (1980) investigated whether learned methods could improve digit span. SF, a long distance runner, learned to encode digit strings as running times (for example, "a good time for the mile") and attained a span of 82 digits. Suppression of rehearsal between presentation and recall by visual interference had no effect, but suppression of auditory rehearsal reduced span by about four items, indicating that most of the items were held in a relatively permanent form immune to such interference. DD, a second subject, who encoded digit groups as dates or other meaningful units, later reached a span of 101 digits. A third subject gave up after achieving only a modest improvement. It may be noted that Dominic O'Brien, at the Second World Memory Championships, twice performed perfectly on the longest sequences presented (100 digits), suggesting that he could easily outdo Ericsson's subjects.

In the case of SF the codings for groups of three to four digits in terms of running times were combined into a larger "retrieval structure" (compare TE's methods described previously). Such a retrieval structure "is a long-term memory structure that is used to make associations with material to be remembered. In effect it serves the function of storing retrieval cues in addressable locations without having to use short-term memory" (Chase & Ericsson, 1981, p. 168). Chase and Ericsson (1982, p. 27) further state that retrieval structures are "a featural description of a location that is generated during encoding ... at recall the features serve

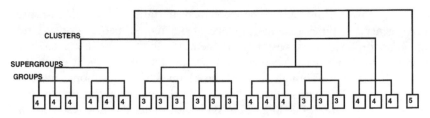

Fig. 2.5. Hypothesised structure of SF's digit recalls.

as a mechanism for activating the trace when the featural description is attended to". The set of locations used in the method of loci is one example of a retrieval structure. SF's eventual retrieval structure consisted of a hierarchical organisation of the sequence of digits, first into groups (usually running times), then into supergroups of three of the running time groups, and finally into clusters of supergroups (pairs of supergroups in the example given by Chase & Ericsson, 1981). Thus, to locate a group within the whole sequence required retention of three features specifying cluster, supergroup, and group position. For a sequence of 80 digits, which SF could consistently retain by the end of his training, Chase and Ericsson hypothesised that SF employed the retrieval structure shown in Fig. 2.5 (the five digits at the end are the rehearsal group held in short-term memory). Thus, the cluster and supergroup features were dichotomous, while the groups had to be labelled as "first", "middle", or "last".

Though this structure provided a simplified method of retaining sequence, as subsequences were only three chunks in length (or four items in some of the groups), it is not entirely clear how and why it provided such a reliable source for memory. One problem is that SF's running codes were imprecise, sometimes inapplicable and sometimes used more than once in a single sequence, and that minimal cues distinguish the positions, unlike the retrieval structure of the method of loci, for example. Another is that the structure had to be used over and over again during a test session, providing ample opportunity for confusions between sequences.

Chase and Ericsson (1981) state that after 100 sessions SF was coding 95% of digit sequences, using running times for 65% of the digit groups, and that he had many subcategories within each running time (such as "a very poor mile time", "an average mile time for the marathon"). These refinements are not apparent in an unpublished tape made by Ericsson of SF in action, admittedly at an early stage of his mnemonic career.[2] In

---

[2]We are grateful for the help of Diane Berry and John Towse in making this tape available to us.

one sequence he mentions no fewer than 12 mile times and 6 two-mile times. Obviously these codes could do no more than aid cueing of exact recall of the digit strings, though the different lengths of the groups within different supergroups would also help to discriminate. For sequences that could not be coded as times, because they included a component of more than 60 seconds, SF often used ages (for example "89.6 years old, very old man"), which have exactly the same problems of imprecision. We discussed these methods with TE who was quite sceptical that they were adequate on their own and suggested that SF must also have had a good memory before he used them (he had, after all, memorised a wide range of running times). However, no evidence of early superiority in memory or expert relatives is suggested.

Though SF's use of codes clearly became more frequent and more fluent with practice, the protocol given by Chase and Ericsson (1981) for Session 39, and the tape referred to previously, both demonstrate a considerable proportion of uncoded sequences, apparently remembered by rote, when SF was recalling sequences of about 20 items. Chase and Ericsson are adamant that he was of average intellectual and memory ability before he began practising his methods (e.g. Ericsson & Chase, 1982, p. 609), but some of the points raised earlier suggest that this may not be completely true. Certainly, the protocol and tape suggest an almost obsessional desire to succeed (a trait also presumably important in his long-distance running achievements) and demonstrate substantial use of an accurate rote memory as well as encoding by running times.

Chase and Ericsson (1981) briefly discuss the problem of reuse of the same retrieval structure. They suggest that the most recent memory trace overwrites earlier ones and is tagged as most recent or distinguished by greater strength. Nevertheless, errors of intrusion from the same position in earlier sequences can occur. One of the experts we have studied, like Ishihara, has developed a variety of locations for the method of loci in order not to reuse a given retrieval structure within an interval of less than about 30 minutes.

These cases primarily illustrate specific, technique-based memory expertise. Ericsson has developed his skilled memory theory largely on the basis of this limited range of tasks. The three principles of the theory are:

1. Meaningful encoding: Information is stored in long-term memory, using knowledge already present.
2. Retrieval structures: These are associated with a group of items and stored with the memory trace for the group. Prior knowledge is used to guide the choice of cues, which will index information in memory to aid retrieval.
3. Speed-up: Encoding and retrieval become much faster with practice.

These principles are very general—they certainly do not provide guidance on how to improve memory on a specific task, other than the general advice to develop structures and to practise. As pointed out previously, the protocol of SF's digit span performance does not completely fit the principles, since recoding using existing knowledge was not always apparent. The key feature of SF's method was *hierarchical* organisation of the digit strings, according to Ericsson's detailed description, yet this is not made explicit in the principles at all. Presumably it is an example of a retrieval structure, but this is certainly not made clear, nor is any account provided of how the hierarchies were developed. Until SF developed this aspect of his method, his results were quite modest. Likewise, TE attained a digit span of only 15 items in the absence of such higher order structures to organise the words he created from groups of three or four digits.

Kliegl, Smith, Heckhausen, and Baltes (1987) have demonstrated that it is only the speeding-up process included in Ericsson's principles that requires extensive practice. The first and second principles can be grasped and used very rapidly. However, the nature of the speeding up, which occurs with practice, as with other skills, is not clearly understood and is quite unaffected by verbal instructions. Hence Ericsson's third principle is little more than a statement of the adage "Practice makes perfect". We will discuss these principles later in relation to the other cases of superior performance described in this chapter.

Bennett (1983) showed that cocktail waitresses were able to remember up to 15 drinks orders with 90% accuracy when they were given in order round a table, and with 80% accuracy when they were scattered between tables. Accuracy was measured by ability to place the drinks in front of the correct customer after a short delay. Waitresses reported that they had developed automatic ability to form interactive images involving features of drink and customer. Some stated that "after a while customers started looking like drinks".

In a detailed study of a single waiter, which investigated the methods used more thoroughly, Ericsson and Polson (1988a, b) examined the ability of a waiter, JC, to remember dinner orders comprising four items for each of up to eight people. JC was tested in a simulated restaurant situation and for each diner was given one of seven possible steak entrées, cooked at one of five possible temperatures, plus one of five possible salad dressings and one of three possible starch dishes. JC stored each type of food for all the diners, rather than all the dishes for the first diner then all for the next diner and so on. Steak entrées were retained in a sequence, taking note of any special patterns such as repetitions. The cooking temperatures were coded as a graph-like pattern, salad dressings were reduced to initial letters and stored as a list, and starches were stored as another list. Information was stored in the order of seating, even when not provided in that order. Tests of JC on a different set of categories (animals, flowers, metals, and times of day) showed he could use a similar system effectively on these, though he did not attain the same level as with the dinner orders. He also showed some superiority compared with controls in recalling uncategorised lists structured in the same form as dinner orders. Thus, he could generalise his skill to a situation where similar structures could be employed.

Though Ericsson believed that JC illustrated the principles given earlier, this is questionable. There is little sign of JC recoding the sequences of items into meaningful chunks, as in Ericsson's first principle, except when a very obvious recoding was apparent, as when initial letters of salad dressings formed a word. The only other type of recoding was the spatial pattern derived for temperatures. No scheme for reducing each possible sequence to a meaningful or learned code is apparent for any of the other items; retrieval was based on sequences of items related to the positions of the diners. To a large extent JC seems merely to have retained simplified sequences and retrieved them in the same order. A major problem with the method described is that it offers no evidence on how JC was able, without advance warning, to report most of the orders, coded by table number, from a test session or evening's work after the end of the proceedings. It is quite unclear how the orders throughout such a session were stored in a sufficiently distinct form to prevent mutual interference and enable recall. Some additional very efficient process is suggested, which JC was unable or unwilling to describe. This could of course have been due to some special innate ability or have become automated, and hence inaccessible, through constant practice. Whichever may be the case, it is clear that something more than Ericsson's three principles is needed to provide a comprehensive explanation and that his case for nurture as the sole factor is far from proven.

Despite these uncertainties, the most plausible conclusion must be that JC's superiority was specific and based on technique.

Rajan Mahadevan

An interesting case described in two recent papers and a book (Biederman et al., 1992; Thompson et al., 1991, 1993) is that of Rajan Mahadevan, who in 1981 recited 31,811 digits of pi, a figure subsequently overtaken by Hideaki Tomoyori, who recited 40,000 digits, but at a much slower rate. Rajan recited the first 10,000 digits at 4.9 per second and overall his rate was 3.5 per second. Tomoyori used a story mnemonic, taking advantage of the fact that the names of single digits in Japanese have a second meaning. His rate of recitation was less than one digit per second.

Thompson et al. (1991) tested Rajan's digit and letter spans with visual and auditory presentation. He recalled 43 digits with auditory presentation and 28 with visual, but only 13 letters under either form of presentation (though even this more modest figure is of course well above the normal letter span). He later achieved a 60 item digit span with visual presentation. His original unpractised digit span before he developed any method of encoding chunks was 15 items. The authors also investigated at what list length his delay time between the end of list presentation and the beginning of recall began to increase, arguing that this would indicate the occurrence of rehearsal before recall and so provide a means of determining how many items he could retain without rehearsal. They found that for lists up to 13 items long Rajan did not increase the delay at all, which suggested that he had a "basic" span of about this length. The normal subjects had a span of seven plus or minus two items, and began to increase their delay before starting to recall once lists exceeded this length. Rajan's basic span was, therefore, highly unusual.

Rajan did not retain longer lists by recoding groups of digits into meaningful chunks of some sort in the manner of Ericsson's first principle, but he seemed to label each digit by its position in the list. The authors refer to this as a form of paired-associate learning, though it does not seem to have been explicit in the same way as in classical paired-associate learning. They state (p. 705): "he keeps track of the location of each digit, while learning sequences of 14 to 17 digits. He then pieces together the shorter sequences to give the complete string" (p. 705). Rajan could give the position of short strings in lists learned earlier in a test session and sometimes he confused sequences from the current list with a similar sequence from the same position in an earlier list. He could also readily recall lists in reverse order, giving locations. In their later discussion, Thompson et al. (1993, p. 28) explain that Rajan "kept track of the location of each digit in the sequence (e.g., Location 13) and not the location in the shorter sequence (e.g., Location 3 in the third group of five). Our observations suggest that he learned shorter sequences ranging from 10 to 15 digits and kept track of the starting location of those sequences". Rajan recalled columns more slowly than rows from a number matrix, taking longer on the middle columns, which demonstrates that he was unlikely to be using a visual image of the actual figures. He stated that he learned rows as units, plus the first column to retain the order of the rows.

Rajan retained for a longer period parts only of sequences that had been tested for immediate recall. On one occasion (Thompson et al., 1993, p. 30) he produced what he claimed were the last 15 numbers from the final 30-digit sequence of the previous day's testing. In fact they were from tests conducted 48 hours previously. It is interesting that the length of this sequence was the same as the estimates of Rajan's digit span without rehearsal, supporting the view that he encoded such sequences as units rather like the normal digit span of about seven items. However, Rajan appeared to be able to retain these units in long-term memory on occasion, unlike normal subjects. Thompson et al. also note that he appeared to be able to hold most of the items from sequences of this size in memory without difficulty while searching for one or two missing items.

The description of Rajan's memory shows that he was able to increase his span with practice but there is no indication that he conformed to Ericsson's principles by converting digit sequences to meaningful chunks or creating special retrieval structures. Furthermore, his span before practice was around 15 items, suggesting that the basic structure of his memory was unusual. Further evidence for qualitative differences between Rajan's memory and that of normal subjects is provided by Biederman et al. (1992), who found that Rajan showed no superiority compared with controls in story recall, recall of the Rey–Osterrieth figure, or recall of word lists with a categorical structure. In fact Rajan, while superior at recalling random word lists, showed no improvement when presented with categorisable lists. The control group showed the usual improvement on the latter and as a result performed somewhat better than Rajan. This failure to make use of meaning to aid recall is reminiscent of S and some of the subjects we have studied ourselves who are described later. Whether it is due to inappropriate use of a habitual method or *inability* to make use of meaning remains unclear. Rajan also showed *inferior* performance to controls in remembering the spatial position and orientation of pictures. His ability to recall or recognise the pictures themselves was not tested, apart from a request five months later to recall the names of the objects depicted. Rajan recalled 10/48, but no comparison data are given so we do not know how good or bad this was. Biederman et al. point out that Rajan's retention of numerical material was much better than this, but Thompson et al. (1993) argue that this was only true when he rehearsed sequences in expectation of delayed testing and that his unrehearsed recall of numbers was much less impressive. Since he is unlikely to have rehearsed the object names, there is no conclusive proof that his memory for these was significantly worse than that for numbers. Nevertheless, the weight of the evidence suggests that Rajan was poor at retaining positional and orientational information. Tests on the Leiter International Performance Scale also showed weaknesses in visuo-motor ability and visual concept formation (Thompson et al., 1993, p. 49), supporting this conclusion. Biederman et al. suggest that their results indicate impairment of the posterior parietal (magnocellular) system discussed in Chapter 3. It is not obvious whether the superiority in sequential memory and inferiority in visuo-spatial ability are coincidental or related in some way.

Rajan's unusual memory was therefore specific and not dependent on explicit techniques. His memory ability was noticed early by his parents, who recalled his ability to remember a large number of car registration numbers in the order in which the cars were parked at a party when he was aged five. His father also demonstrated unusual memory, learning large sections of Shakespeare and quantities of medical information, and his brother showed some signs of superior memory ability. A more distant relative, Srinivasa Ramanujan, was a famous mathematician and at an early age could recite pi to many decimal places.

Rajan's most impressive performances were in learning long lists of numbers, such as large matrices and above all his mastery of pi to over 30,000 places. Details of his performance on this material are presented by Thompson et al. (1993). Table 2.4 shows his time per digit to learn matrices up to 20×20 items, compared with controls, and Table 2.5 shows time to recall rows and columns of a 6×6 matrix (data derived from Thompson et al., 1993, pp. 54–55). These results show his immense superiority and also confirm his report that he encodes by rows plus the first column. Even in matrices of 20×20 items, his recall showed no

TABLE 2.4

Times Per Digit in Seconds to Learn Matrices of Different Sizes for Control Subjects and for Rajan (Derived from Fig. 4.1 of Thompson et al., 1993)

				Matrix size				
	5×5	6×6	7×7	9×9	10×10	12×12	14×14	20×20
Controls	6.7	8.5	12.3	13.8	–	–	–	–
Rajan	2.0	1.3	1.7	2.4	2.8	3.2	4.1	5.6

TABLE 2.5

Times in Seconds to Recall Rows and Columns of a 6×6 Matrix for Control Subjects and Rajan (Derived from Fig. 4.2 of Thompson et al., 1993)

	1	2	3	4	5	6
Rows						
Controls	3.5	5.5	8.0	12.5	7.5	4.0
Rajan	2.0	2.0	3.0	1.5	2.0	2.0
Columns						
Controls	16.0	30.0	29.0	37.5	45.0	29.0
Rajan	2.5	12.0	11.0	17.0	20.0	15.0

evidence for division of the rows into separate chunks separated by pauses.

Rajan was able to recall completely 8 out of 12 matrices (sizes ranging from 5 × 5 to 14 × 14) which he had seen six months earlier. However, the authors suspected that he might have rehearsed these in expectation of a delayed test, so after a further six months they tested him on the new matrices which had been presented at the first delayed recall test, to examine further his ability to retain matrices seen before. They argued that Rajan had less reason to expect a further test of delayed retention and in fact he could only recall one (5 × 5) matrix, though his ability to recognise which matrices he had seen before was still much superior to that of control subjects. The authors suggest (p. 141) that "his memory over long retention intervals is clearly not as spectacular as the memory reported for Shereshevskii (Luria, 1975) and documented for VP". This may be unjust since Rajan was asked to recall several number matrices, which was likely to have caused mutual interference.

A large part of Thompson et al.'s book is devoted to studying Rajan's ability to find information in his memorised representation of pi over the first 10,000 places. He had learned this from a display consisting of rows of 100 digits divided into blocks of 10 within rows and also into blocks of 10 rows separated by a blank line, which therefore demarcated 1000 digits. A page contained 5000 digits. Experiments on his speed of locating digits in specified locations, or specified rows, or chunks of 5 digits from different points in blocks of 10 demonstrated that Rajan's internal representation was structured like the original display and searched as if it were being read line by line. For example, he could locate the first 5 digits from a block of 10 more easily than the second 5. The authors suggest that the blocks of 10 digits are like logogens (Morton, 1970), but meaningless, being "chunked" solely by rote learning (p. 135): "We think the efficacy of rote learning has been constantly underestimated when discussing such concepts as chunks or logogens. These data from Rajan tend to underscore that point. More specifically, Rajan's 10-digit chunks are almost totally bereft of relationships to meaningful material. Nevertheless they have all the characteristics of Morton's logogens."

Rajan neatly demonstrates the results of initial ability combined with powerful motivation to succeed. The span experiments suggest that both his digit and letter span were of unusual length, but it is only for digits that he has developed the skill of encoding longer sequences for immediate recall and of learning very long sequences. Clearly methods of achieving similar feats with letter strings could be devised, but memory feats traditionally involve numbers and Rajan has a special interest in these, so there has been little incentive for him to broaden his achievements to encompass other types of material.

Bubbles P

Bubbles P is a professional gambler studied by Ceci et al. (1992). He was noted for his ability to recall digits backward: Ceci et al. found that he could recall 15 to 20 digits in reverse order, when presented with them as fast as 4 per second (it is not clearly stated but this presentation was presumably visual). A 30-second distraction task of mental arithmetic reduced his backward span to 10 digits and a visual distraction task reduced the backward span to 12. Forward recall was of the same order as backward and he could produce both to the same input and indeed he could start recall at any point in the sequence and still produce a span of around 20 digits. His delayed recall 30 minutes later was non-existent unless he was warned at presentation, when he could produce correct or nearly correct recall.

There was no evidence that Bubbles P was using any standard mnemonic method. When asked how he did the task, he claimed it was quite simple. He simply saw the numbers horizontally in front of his eyes (Ceci, personal communication). However, if asked to give a digit at a named position "it took him several seconds to do this, as he appeared to mentally count digits, rather than having an immediate spatial readout" (Ceci et al., 1992, p. 175).

Ceci et al. tested Bubbles P on a number of memory tasks in order to identify the boundaries of his skill. On the Atkinson–Shiffrin keeping track task (see the earlier discussion of TE) he performed slightly below the average level of a control group. On face recognition he performed at around the 75th percentile, so was not exceptional. However, he did insist on a faster rate of presentation than the standard three seconds per item and no test is reported of whether this affected his performance. On word recognition he performed perfectly with visual presentation of 50 words (compared with a normal mean for his age group of 45.75 with a standard deviation of 3.62), but only at an average level when presentation was auditory. He showed average ability in reproducing the positions of a series of lights.

He was given Luria's 50-digit matrix, which Luria used with S (12 rows of 4 items each and one of 2 items). This was also given to VP and TE. Results for all four subjects are in Table 2.6, having been omitted from the discussions earlier in order to make comparisons at this point. It should be noted that Ceci et al. give the same figures for VP and TE, those for TE being erroneous, and do not include TE in their discussion. Later, we discuss results derived from a different matrix given to VP, TE, and several other subjects studied subsequently by us.

The data in Table 2.6 show that the study times were similar for VP and Bubbles P, but S, SF, and TE were much faster. Bubbles P recalled

TABLE 2.6
Times in Seconds to Recall Luria's 50-item Number Matrix for Four Mnemonists

	S	SF	VP	TE	Bubbles	Controls[3]
Study time	180	187[1]	390	144	424	860
Recall whole	40	43	41.5	53.8	16[2]	66
Column 3	80	41	58.1	72.2	50.6	90
Column 2	25	41	39.4	43.2	35.5	66
Column 2 upwards	30	47	39.7	47.7	18.0	76

[1] a year later SF took 81 seconds; [2] this figure is for Bubbles' second recall; [3] four subjects reported by Ericsson and Chase (1982).

the whole matrix more rapidly than the other subjects but only on his second recall, given because the pace of the first was constrained by making a video recording at the same time. Hence, no proper comparison with the other subjects is possible. Times for recall of specific columns in descending or ascending order are similar in all cases, apart from Bubbles P's recall of Column 2 in ascending order, which was much faster than the other subjects and his other times for column recall. This was probably an example of his facility at reverse recall, having already recalled the column in descending order. Column recall took about the same time as recall of the whole matrix in all subjects, suggesting that none of them was reading from a visual image, in which case reading 13 numbers should take less time than reading 50 numbers. The times obtained strongly suggest that a representation of the whole matrix had to be searched to retrieve the required numbers from a single column. However, Ceci et al. (p. 179), while making this point for S and VP, claim that "in contrast" Bubbles P demonstrated faster recall of columns and therefore was reading from a visual image. In fact, the only case where his column recall was faster is the ascending recall of Column 2 discussed above, which is explicable in terms of his facility with reversed recall.

In a further argument for their view that Bubbles retained a visual image, the authors write (p. 179), "The rapidity with which he could recall digits in any location compared to the long times required by S and VP ... strongly suggest that Bubbles had a spatial code that enabled him to read out digits in any location. This interpretation is supported by his own self-report; he claimed to 'see' the matrix 'vividly'." However, no data are given for speed of recalling single specified digits (if this is what the above statement refers to), nor were the other subjects given any such tests, so the basis of the claim is obscure.

Bubbles was also given a task of learning playing card matrices and performed this accurately in less study time than he took with the digit matrix. He could also specify cards in named cells, without an empty matrix visible. He recognised a repeated card matrix after six weeks (from the first and last rows, but no test of complete recall was carried out), and demonstrated partial retention of another matrix over 30 minutes of digit and card tests (no detailed figures are given).

IQ tests suggested that Bubbles was of average ability with exceptional performance only on digit recall. Ceci et al. argue that this case suggests that memory is highly context- (actually material-)dependent, since his superiority was only apparent on numerical material (including playing cards). This is not completely true as his word recognition performance was perfect with visual presentation and face recognition was well above average. Since recognition of auditorily presented words was only average, there is an indication that Bubbles' visual memory was unusual. The digit span tests seem to have been visually presented and no auditory tests of number recall were carried out (note that Binet's subjects and Rajan demonstrated considerable differences in the two modalities). Whether Bubbles' superiority was associated with numbers or visual presentation, either possibility indicates a specific area of superiority, which Ceci et al. wish to argue is typical of other mnemonists also. A major theme of this book is that this is an oversimplification and that both general and specific memory superiority can be observed.

The implication of Ceci et al.'s discussion, though they are not explicit on this issue, is that experience and practice are the key variables in determining memory superiority. They do not, however, appear to have questioned Bubbles about the origins of his ability. Was he aware of it early, did he develop it over time during his gambling career, and did any of his relatives have similar ability? Nor do the reported experiments enable close analysis of the nature of his skills. As already pointed out, no test of auditory digit span was given and letter span was not tested. Why was recognition memory for words so much worse with auditory than with visual presentation? On the current evidence it is difficult to draw any firm conclusions about the nature of Bubbles' memory ability.

Comparison of "Numerical" Mnemonists

The remainder of this chapter will consider a number of further examples of unusual memory for material of a specific type. Before considering these it will be useful to take an overview of the different performances that have been described so far in order to compare the achievements of the individuals who have been described. In several cases no control data were provided by the authors of the reports, so it is useful to set performance in the context of other reported results in order to gain an idea of just how good it may have been. Furthermore, such comparisons will indicate the highest levels of performance that have been achieved, whether any single individual consistently outperforms all others, and the degree to which performance across different experts reaches a similar level. Such comparisons would be still more informative if they could be made across a number of tasks, so that it could be seen whether superior performance by a single individual is task specific or not. Unfortunately, however, the comparisons that can be made from the data available before we carried out our own studies are extremely limited.

The evidence surveyed has been very varied in nature. Much of it is fragmentary or the detail provided is very unsatisfactory. Different researchers have used different tasks and different measures, and early researchers were often cavalier in their experimental control and provision of normative data. The point has already been made that extensive knowledge of unusual detail about a topic or of little-known topics, without evidence of the time and methods used to acquire such knowledge, is largely irrelevant to the issues which are of interest in the present context. Assessment of memory ability in such cases requires measurement of the time for which the material was studied in order to achieve recall or recognition.

In many other cases a relatively short delay intervenes between learning of the material and the memory test, but assessment of delayed retention would be more informative as it matches more closely the general understanding of the notion of memory ability. Alternatively the amount retained from material exposed for a fixed interval can be measured; again short delays are commonly imposed in such studies which means that performance reflects mainly the speed and efficiency of the initial encoding of the material. Though retention over longer intervals may well depend on the efficiency of such encoding, additional processes are likely to be involved. Therefore, measures of retention are highly desirable.

Numerical material has been by far the most popular medium employed. This has both advantages and disadvantages. The main advantage is that such material is relatively culture free and results should be comparable across subjects from different backgrounds and speaking different languages. However, even with numbers it has been shown that the names employed in a specific language will affect short-term recall (Ellis & Hennelly, 1980; Hoosain & Salili, 1987; Stigler, Lee, & Stevenson, 1986). The disadvantage of the popularity of numbers in memory experiments is that unwarranted generalisations about memory ability may be drawn on the basis of a very restricted body of data. For example, it may be that memory superiority for a specific type of material does occur for numbers but not for other types of material. Furthermore, even with numbers, experimenters have rarely used identical test conditions or measures of performance, and the absence of detail about methodology may make it impossible to decide whether or not two experiments were run under identical or even similar conditions.

Can we therefore make any useful comparisons between different individuals which point to any general conclusions about the range of ability and maximum possible attainments on specific tasks? Not surprisingly, it is impossible to find any tasks that have been used consistently over all the individuals who have been described. The tasks that have been most widely used have been numerical and Table 2.7 summarises the available

TABLE 2.7
Available Comparisons between Experts in Time to Learn Number Sequences

Number of Items	Name (Rank Order)	Time (secs)
20	Ishihara	11.4
	Rückle	17.2
25	Inaudi	45.0
	Diamandi	180.0
5 × 5 matrix	Rückle	20.2[***]
	Finkelstein	c.18.0
	Inaudi	45.0
	Diamandi	150.0
48	Ishihara	39.6
	Rückle	52.4
6 × 8 matrix[*]	Subject H	72.0
	Subject C	160.0
	Subject I	185.0
	TE	191.8
	TM	207.0
	VP	246.0
7 × 7 matrix	Rajan	84.0
4 × 12 matrix (+2 extra items) (Luria's matrix)	SF	87.0[****]
	TE	144.0
	S	180.0
	VP	390.0
	Bubbles P	424.0
200[**]	Arnould	45 minutes
	Diamandi	75 minutes
204[**]	Ishihara	9 minutes 30 seconds
	Rückle	20 minutes 30 seconds

[*]Results for Subjects H, C, and I are reported in Chapter 5 and results for TM in Chapter 4. [**]Times include recall time. Ishihara took 5 minutes 54 seconds and Rückle 18 minutes 11 seconds (later reduced to 7 minutes) for learning only. These times are not available for Arnould and Diamandi. [***]Later this was reduced to 12.7 seconds. [****]See Table 2.6.

evidence already discussed, plus a few findings from our own studies reported later; tasks have been grouped into very similar, though not identical, sets to facilitate comparison.

The results demonstrate clearly the very high degree of expertise demonstrated by Ishihara, who is by far the fastest learner in all comparisons which involve him. The results also show the very wide range of variation, even within this group of experts.

Ishihara depended on a well-learned strategy (imagery plus the method of loci) to which Japanese is particularly well-suited. He was also good at learning word lists, using a similar strategy. These tasks are the type of tasks on which strategic methods are extremely effective. In fact, all the subjects featuring in Table 2.7, with the exception of Rajan, seem to have employed some form of strategy. It can be safely concluded that, apart from very rare individuals, long unstructured lists of material can only be learned and retained effectively through a method of semanticisation and structuring (providing retrieval cues, in Ericsson's terminology). Even Rajan, an individual with an unusual natural ability to retain a particular type of material, was inferior to Ishihara, whose performance depended on strategy. It does not, of course, follow that, in the absence of strategies, no individual differences exist in the ability to memorise numerical or other unstructured material, nor that strategists will be the best performers on every type of task, since their strategies are not universally applicable. Unfortunately, no relevant data are available to make a comparison of performance over several tasks for a number of subjects. Our own study described in Chapter 5 will attempt to remedy this deficiency.

The remainder of this chapter collects together a number of examples of superior memory performance in specific tasks, with a particular type of material, or demonstrated by individuals from a special population.

CJ

There have been many reports of individuals (usually male) with an extreme facility for acquiring foreign languages after puberty, such as Edward Gibbon and George Borrow.

One such individual who has been studied more systematically is CJ, a subject investigated by Novoa et al. (1988). He studied French at university but also learned, usually "in a matter of weeks", German, Arabic, Spanish, and Italian, to a level at which native speakers agreed that his ability and accent were close to that of native speakers. Other tested aspects of CJ's verbal memory showed exceptional performance. While doing the WAIS digit–symbol substitution task he learned the complete code and was able to repeat it 20 minutes later. He could still give most of the paired associates from the Wechsler memory scale two weeks after doing the test, and scored at the 99th percentile on immediate and delayed recall of prose. There was some evidence for a weakness in visuo-spatial ability, though it was not marked. He was left-handed, which may be relevant to the interpretation of his abilities. No doubt his ability had improved with his experience in acquiring new languages, but the account clearly demonstrates unusual verbal memory ability. His ability to acquire incidental details like accent (normally extremely difficult for the adult learner), without any apparent deliberate effort, suggests that his learning differed considerably from that of the average second language learner. No information is given on his early abilities or those of his relatives.

In summary, CJ's memory ability was specific, not dependent on delib-erate technique, and qualitatively different from that of normal second language learners. There is no evidence on his early ability or that of relatives.

Unusual Visual Memory

Gummerman and Gray (1971) describe a case of a 19-year-old student who displayed unusual ability to recall pictures seen for only 30 seconds. Though no control data are provided, the amount of detail in her descrip-tions seems highly unusual, but the authors are clear that no eidetic imagery was involved. On five other memory tasks (matrices containing numbers, dots, or geometric patterns, reproduction of random shapes, recall of prose and poetry, recalling a letter from a probed position in a nine-letter display shown for 200 milliseconds, and recalling multi-item arrays), the authors report that performance was not remarkable; no data are given and it is difficult to draw any firm conclusions from this report.

Coltheart and Glick (1974) described a female subject, named Sue d'Onim by them, who could visualise words and sentences, then spell them backwards. They believed that she had superior imagery ability. However, Cowan et al. (Cowan, Braine, & Leavitt, 1985; Cowan and Leavitt, 1982, 1987; Cowan, Leavitt, Massaro, & Kent, 1982) have described subjects who developed this skill with practice, and Ericsson and Faivre (1988, p. 466) argue that this "casts doubt on the need for unusual basic capacities as prerequisites". This argument ignores some points about the Coltheart and Glick study. Sue d'Onim showed excep-tional ability to report items from Sperling's (1960) task in which a matrix of letters and numbers is flashed briefly and subjects have to report from a cued line of the matrix. She scored 7.44 items correct on average, compared with control subjects' average of 4.76. She acquired information from the display much more rapidly and reached a higher ceiling than the controls. These abilities are reminiscent of some of

Finkelstein's achievements reported previously. There is no reason to suppose that practice in backward spelling develops such an ability. Unfortunately, we do not know whether the subjects tested by Cowan and his associates possessed it, because they did not carry out the test. A more plausible explanation of Sue d'Onim's performance on both tasks is that her visual images were, in Coltheart and Glick's words, "abnormally resistant to disruption".

Stromeyer and Psotka (1970) report a subject who was shown a random dot stereogram to one visual field and another to the other visual field after a delay. This subject was able to combine the two images, one memoric and the other perceptual, stereoscopically and report the resulting figure in depth. She claimed that the task was "ridiculously easy", even though it requires storage of the exact dot pattern over a lengthy period. Simpler patterns could be combined after an interval of three days.

Three Autistic Children

Autistic children sometimes show unusual memory for a particular type of material.

Elly (Bogyo & Ellis, 1988; Park, 1967) had virtually perfect memory for any route she had travelled and for the position of objects in the home, even before she had names for the objects. Though her language ability was poor, she could often repeat large parts of conversations she had heard about topics unfamiliar to her. She could not understand metaphor and pragmatic aspects of language; she was obsessed with discovering regular physical patterns in the world, in language and especially in numbers, on which she had accumulated a vast store of information. She could multiply large numbers quickly and scored at the 95th percentile on Raven's matrices, doing the tasks very rapidly. Bogyo and Ellis (1988) suggest that Elly became obsessed with physical order to compensate for her problems in understanding other aspects of human life. However, her memory for routes at least was noted as early as two years of age, and it is equally plausible that both her strengths and weaknesses were present from birth. Her pattern of abilities reads like a more extreme form of Shereshevskii's memory.

An autistic boy, Paul, described by Lucci, Fein, Holevas, and Kaplan (1988), demonstrated a similar pattern of remembering routes and events from an early age, around two to three years. His paired associate performance was at the 84th percentile but his memory for a story was only at the 5th percentile. He too (like CJ) remembered the digit–symbol pairs from the WISC, though he only saw them for 90 seconds and only completed one line of the test. His main expertise was in music, in which he became interested at a very early age. At the age of seven he used to play a game with a graduate music student in which each would play an improvised sequence, after which the other immediately tried to reproduce it. Paul could reproduce longer sequences than his opponent.

A third autistic case with exceptional memory was studied by Waterhouse (1988). JD had detailed knowledge of popular music, routes he had travelled, and the birthdays of all his acquaintances. His visual memory was especially good. He used to play the popular memory game in which 64 pictures are laid out face down in random order, then each player turns up two pictures on each turn, attempting to find matching pairs by using information recalled from earlier attempts; each time a pair is successfully located the player takes another turn. JD would lay out the pictures, take the first turn and clear the board, remembering where he had placed each pair. Though no control data are provided, if this was a consistent achievement, there is little doubt that it demonstrates unusual memory. His performance on the WISC block design task was also quite exceptional. He could replace 10 objects on a board after seeing the board for only two seconds, a performance unique among all the subjects tested by the experimenter. JD was, however, poor at recognising faces and in language skills.

Some researchers have argued that cases such as these illustrate only the effect of obsessional practice at tasks, which enables these subjects to avoid social contact. However, in each of these cases some evidence, usually anecdotal it must be admitted, suggests unusual memory ability early in life. The studies also demonstrate exceptional performance on properly controlled tasks, which would neither have been familiar to the subjects nor part of their well-practised routines.

These subjects provide examples of specific, qualitatively different memories not dependent on techniques, which are apparent early in life. Evidence on abilities of relatives is not normally available.

Musical Savants

Musical savants are those possessing musical skills markedly out of proportion to other intellectual abilities. Judd (1988) surveyed 18 cases in the literature. Such savants typically play by ear (many are blind), commonly possess absolute pitch, and often have musical memories exceptional even in comparison with skilled musicians. They demonstrate sensitivity to musical structure and rules, performing better on structured than on random sequences (Charness, 1988; Miller, 1989; Sloboda, Hermelin, & O'Connor, 1985), though their performance on the latter is often better than that of normal subjects. Though frequently accused of rigid mechanical performance, their cognitive structures appear comparable to those of normal musicians, but restricted to the musical domain. Their skill has often been attributed to intensive practice and/or the reinforcement obtained from discovering an area of competence. However, organic factors may also be implicated. Lucci et al. (1988) reported that in the case of Paul (discussed earlier) there was an abnormal EEG in the right temporal region, known to be involved in tonal memory and timbre discrimination. They suggest hyperfunctioning and the possibility that dedicated cortical areas may be reorganised during a sensitive period. There is also often a family history of musicality and multiple causation is likely.

Concert Pianists

A number of studies of the learning of high ability concert pianists have been reported (Chaffin & Imreh, 1994; Manturzewska, 1960; Miklaszewski, 1989; Wicinski, 1950). The more recent of these have involved detailed recording and analysis of the exact passages practised, as well as verbal commentaries. The evidence indicates that the organisation of practice reflects both the structure and difficulty of the piece, with more difficult passages being broken down into smaller sections and receiving more attention. Over time the difference between easy and difficult sections, in terms of the size of practice unit, the amount of practice required, and the number of cues needed to elicit performance, is reduced.

Miklaszewski's subject, subsequently a professional concert pianist, reported that he first tried to build up an internal representation of the piece in its various aspects, quickly supporting this by imagining how his hands would perform it; remedial action would then be taken, employing means–end analysis, until a master plan for performance was finally achieved.

Chaffin and Imreh's subject, also a professional pianist, indicated a hierarchy of retrieval cues, with a shift in attention from the basic skills required for technical mastery to considerations of interpretation and expression in the later stages of practice. It is likely that these stages are not clearly distinct but partially overlapping and may vary somewhat between performers. Musical memory is a particularly interesting example due to its multidimensionality, incorporating both motor and cognitive elements, plus technical and expressive components.

The Memory of Actors

Actors have to memorise the exact words of large quantities of material, rather than retaining meaning only, as is the more usual demand on memory. Hence, they are of special interest in the study of memory expertise. Do all actors start with an unusually good memory? Do they develop it by training? Do they use special methods? These are just some of the questions that arise.

Osborn (1902, p. 184) quotes a letter from one actor who claimed that actors could acquire by long experience the art of rote learning or "winging" a part very rapidly. A man (this actor claimed that few women could master the technique!) might do this by reading a part "as he came off the stage at every scene and fixing mechanically upon his memory the shape of the written part, the very hand-writing, the position of each speech upon the paper, the sequence of the same, and all the details which would present themselves to his physical eye". Barlow (1951, p. 170ff.) also claimed that actors visua-lised scripts and learned by rote, often to the extent that delivery was automatic, so they could be thinking of something quite different while speaking the part. He quotes an article in *John O'Londons Weekly* (1 March 1940), which tells of one actor who calculated his income tax while delivering a lengthy speech from *Cyrano de Bergerac*!

Experimental studies of actors were carried out by Oliver and Ericsson (1986) and by Intons-Peterson and Smyth (1987). The former study showed that actors could be cued by even a single word to retrieve from large parts and that, where several parts were known, it was not a great advantage to be pre-cued as to which part to search. Hence, to the surprise of the actors themselves, a large body of material was learned quite rapidly to a level at which it was simultaneously available very quickly in response to minimal cues. Intons-Peterson and Smyth compared students from a Department of Theatre and Drama, with at least four years' experience of theatre groups, who were considered to be quick memorisers of scripts, with novices drawn from a psychology course. Their subjects learned two prose passages (191 and 243 words long), and were recorded while rehearsing the passages aloud. Words that began paragraphs and sentences were rehearsed more; experts varied the number of rehearsals more than novices. Rehearsed chunks corresponded closely to sentences, though novices tended to attempt larger chunks than did experienced actors. After 20 minutes' rehearsal, subjects recalled about 95% and still retained about 84% four days after their exposure to the passages (they had attempted recall twice in the intervening period). Little interference was observed between the two passages learned.

The evidence quoted so far suggests that rote learning of scripts is both possible and may become very rapid with practice, to an extent that experienced actors can rely on it to serve their needs. However, in a fasci-nating series of studies of actors' learning ability and methods, Noice and

Noice (Noice, 1991, 1992, 1993; Noice & Noice, 1993, 1996) have come to very different conclusions.

They demonstrate that, by normal standards, actors' memory ability is astonishing. VP's ability to recall "The War of the Ghosts" after one reading was impressive but would rate very poorly for an actor required to reproduce a speech verbatim. The Noices' research shows that highly experienced actors do not memorise in the normal sense of that term. They read through a script, interpreting the causes of the precise words uttered, the intention behind them and the underlying meaning; this process produces perfect memory as a by-product. The difference between this approach and that of a mnemonic expert was highlighted in a comparison of the learning of a script by a group of actors and the "memory man" Harry Lorayne (Noice & Noice, 1996). Normally it is assumed that reading for meaning results in memory for gist rather than literal memory, but actors' effort after meaning produces exact recall.

In one sense the method actors adopt is an example of Ericsson's skilled memory processes. Utterances are translated into another form, consisting of intentions and complex meanings, then connected into a causal chain (a retrieval structure). This skill must develop with practice, though Noice and Noice have yet to report any study of the development of the skill. Other obvious questions concern the generality of such a method. The studies all concentrate on the learning of dialogue, where the method is particularly appropriate. Presumably it is also applicable to longer speeches, so in principle it has valuable lessons to offer for the study of other forms of written material.

It is not entirely clear why the evidence from the latter studies is so different from that quoted earlier. The study by Intons-Peterson and Smyth involved relatively inexperienced actors compared with those in the Noices' studies; the experimental material and procedure tended to encourage rote learning, which may explain some of the differences in results. However, the anecdotal evidence from experienced actors suggests that rote learning is also employed, contrary to the whole thrust of the Noices' argument.

Ballet Dancers

Allard and Starkes (1991) discuss the memory of motor-skill experts such as ballet dancers. More skilled performers were able to make more use of structure which followed conventional rules to aid memory. An adult principal dancer with the National Ballet company was able to perform a new 96-step sequence after only one viewing. Verbal labelling and hand movements were used to code the sequence into units.

CONCLUSIONS

We have now covered studies of superior memory performance prior to our own more detailed investigations, which will be described from Chapter 4 onwards. In the next chapter we will consider this evidence in relation to some of the questions raised in Chapter 1. First, we will address the issue of whether this evidence suggests that memory superiority always depends on learned methods, as has been strongly argued by Ericsson. We will argue that such a view is too narrow and that a number of indications occur in the literature suggesting natural variation in memory ability, and consequently occasional cases of superior natural memory ability can be observed.

This argument encounters the objection that current views of the structure of memory favour a modular system in the brain, with several distinct subsystems handling different types of material or memory. If true, this could rule out the possibility of a single scale of memory ability. We will therefore consider the evidence for this view and argue that it is not incompatible with the existence of general parameters of efficiency underlying a wide range of memory performance.

We will also consider the relations between memory and other cognitive abilities, specifically intelligence and imagery (these relations being the final question raised at the end of Chapter 1). There is little relevant evidence on these questions from the studies of superior memory we have described so far, but a range of other evidence is available and will be considered before we begin to address these questions in our own later studies.

Chapter 3, therefore, will try to set the studies of superior memory within the context of recent memory research in general, and to consider some of the related theoretical issues from a wider perspective than simply that of superior memory performance.

3 The Nature and Nurture of Memory

The purposes of this chapter are:

1. To evaluate the argument that superior memory performance depends on learned techniques.
2. To review the evidence which suggests that memory consists of several independent systems, in order to assess whether this would preclude the possibility of identifying general memory superiority over a wide range of tasks.
3. To review evidence on the relation between general intelligence and memory in order to decide whether these depend on separate psychological functions or whether memory ability is closely related to intelligence.
4. To review the evidence on the relation between imagery abilities and memory, to determine the role played by imagery in superior memory and in particular whether superior imagery ability is necessary or sufficient for superior memory ability and whether the nature of the task and individual differences in imagery ability are influential in determining the role of imagery in memory performance.

TRAINING OR TALENT?

The cases described in Chapter 2 combine to demonstrate that superior memory performance often does depend on specially developed methods (Inaudi, Diamandi, Arnould, Ishihara, Finkelstein, TE, SF, DD, probably

JC) or sometimes possibly on a more general early training in a particular style of information processing (VP). Even in some of these cases there is reasonable doubt that techniques are the whole story and in several others it is extremely unlikely that this is the case (probably Coltheart and Click's subject, Gummerman and Gray's subject, S, Aitken, CJ, Rajan, Bubbles P, possibly Elly, Paul, and JD, though practice is likely to have been important in these last three cases). Most of the cases in the latter group show specific strengths and weaknesses, suggesting that some qualitative change in brain organisation is present. The only example of general memory superiority appears to be Aitken (and possibly TE).

This conclusion is clearly at odds with the view that all exceptional memory performance described in the literature can be accounted for by the employment of special methods (Ericsson & Faivre, 1988). These authors argue that (p. 466):

1. Superior performance due to practice cannot be distinguished from superior performance that is claimed to depend on exceptional innate ability. (Of course, if taken seriously, this claim would make it impossible for them to defend their thesis or for others to refute it, but they seem uninhibited by this consequence!)
2. Performance by supposedly untrained memory experts is limited to specific types of stimuli and cannot therefore be ascribed to a general innate ability.
3. Trained subjects cannot provide more explicit descriptions of how they achieve their performance than subjects whose achievements are claimed to be due to natural ability. Therefore, lack of explanation from the performer is no guarantee that the achievement is due to innate ability.
4. "to prove exceptionality, the skill must be one that is not attainable ... through practice".

Refutation of the second claim by demonstration of unusual memory ability over a wide range of tasks, especially if some of these were not clearly amenable to practised methods, would necessarily refute the first claim also. We will be discussing later some relevant case studies to add to the rather meagre evidence deployed so far and we will also begin to develop objective criteria, which converge to discriminate, on behavioural grounds rather than self-report, between subjects who can describe their methods and those who claim not to be using well-practised methods.

The second claim is true only if a restricted range of evidence is considered. Even Ericsson seems to admit that superior performance can sometimes occur on unpractised tasks, when he allows the possibility of generalisation of a skill to a novel task. After referring to our study of TE who demonstrated ability over several tasks, and his own demonstration that JC could apply his method to material other than dinner orders, Ericsson (1988, p. 174) states, "I am quite optimistic that we will significantly improve our general understanding of transfer by making further detailed analysis of transfer of skilled memory performance." Ericsson and Polson (1988a) are somewhat more explicit, arguing (p. 69) that some methods are transferable between situations: "we would like to focus on the existence of transferable processes that can improve memory in a wide range of situations". Elsewhere, however, Ericsson points out that generalisation did not occur from digit span to letter span in his studies, so he only invokes generalisation when faced with performance that is not explicable in terms of direct practice. The claim seems to require that superior performance can only occur on tasks that permit the use of strategies. We have provided several examples above of superior performance on tasks that were not well practised or immediately amenable to strategies (Aitken, Gummerman, and Gray's subject, CJ) and will provide others later.

While we have no quarrel with the conclusion to Ericsson's third point that absence of explanation of a method is no guarantee that no method exists, we contest the claim that there is no relation between training and ability to describe a method. Clearly, a subject whose performance depends on natural ability cannot describe a method, since no special method exists, and, while many trained subjects can give detailed descriptions of their methods, others cannot. However, a detailed description of a method would normally seem to imply some learned component to the memory performance. Ericsson's claim is odd in the face of his detailed presentation of explanations of their methods by SF, DD, and JC. Perhaps the claim being made is that anyone who can match the performance of these subjects would necessarily be using a method and therefore be able to describe it. This may well be true for digit spans of the order of those produced by SF and DD, but Rajan was unable to provide any clear explanation of how he achieved his "basic" span of 15 items, and even his account of how he achieved longer spans was less than fully explicit. The same is true of Bubbles P. Furthermore, we will be offering examples of other tasks where some subjects provided descriptions of how they achieved exceptional performance whereas others could not, and we will demonstrate that these two groups could also be differentiated on other criteria.

Ericsson et al.'s fourth point that a skill is only exceptional if it cannot be attained by practice is clearly illogical. First, level of skill is assessed by comparison with norms; method of attaining the skill is irrelevant. Second, excellence in any field can be achieved by more than one route. If a skill can be demonstrated without practice it does not follow that there is no other way to acquire it. Nor, if a skill can be acquired through practice, does it follow that everyone who possesses it must have acquired it in the same way. Third, some people need less practice than others on any task, and this indicates that some pre-practice differences exist. When one person requires little practice and another requires prolonged practice, clearly the achievement of the faster learner is not due solely to practice. Furthermore, Ericsson appears to wish to assert that practice provides a sufficient explanation, without considering that certain abilities may be necessary prerequisites for employing and benefiting from the techniques employed. Again, we will later describe cases of superior performance, some of which depend on technique and some of which appear to occur without such methods.

Ericsson's Principles of Skilled Learning

Though not accepting Ericsson's claims about the all-embracing explanatory power of learned methods in producing superior memory performance, we still need to consider his analysis of the key features of learned methods and decide whether they adequately describe the methods generally used. To recapitulate, Ericsson and Chase (1982) proposed three principles of skilled memory: semanticisation (i.e. use of long-term memory to encode meaningless material by associating it with already known information), use of retrieval structures, and speed-up of both input and retrieval. It has already been pointed out that these processes seem barely adequate to represent Ericsson's own data on SF and JC. This may be because the principles are not a satisfactory account of the operations of memory skill (perhaps due to the incomplete nature of the accounts provided by the subjects) or because other processes are important, which are not encompassed by Ericsson's principles. These principles depend heavily on information derived from subjects' reports of their methods, backed by evidence from other features of their performance. Our own work similarly has made extensive use of such data. Ericsson and Simon (1980, 1984) claim that the validity of an introspective report depends on various factors concerning the relation of the verbalisations to the processing task; in some cases the verbalisations may alter the task process. Critical factors are the time interval between verbalisation and task, and the degree of recoding, interpretation, or inference involved. Subjects can only report accurately on information in focal attention. Reports will be most accurate when concurrent and direct to a specific probe. In the current context, general accounts by subjects of their methods may be useful guides to designing further tests, while accounts of specific methods employed in specific tasks will gain more credence when supported by objective evidence, such as the nature of the errors committed.

What of the other subjects we have described, where the account available gives sufficient detail to compare with Ericsson's principles? S encoded meaningless material as meaningful images and used the method of loci to provide a retrieval structure. He probably carried out these operations quickly but no concrete data are available, largely because S insisted on adequate time between items to construct his representations and no test was carried out on how quickly he could operate if required.

VP provides evidence of semanticisation in storing numbers as dates and nonsense syllables as words, but no explanation is given of his method with the Atkinson–Shiffrin keeping track task or with story recall. Nor is there any indication in Hunt and Love's account as to how VP organised larger structures for retrieval.

TE consistently used information he had in long-term memory (the digit–letter alphabet) to encode numbers and could do this very rapidly. He relied primarily on association of images to retain sequences (as in the Atkinson–Shiffrin task and matrix recall), plus some prelearned structures (such as his associations to numbers: 1— eat, 2—inn, etc.). To learn names to faces TE employed a method which is quite widely used, originally due to Lorayne (1958). A prominent feature of the face is selected and exaggerated, so that some associate is evoked which can be connected readily to the name (e.g. big ears—oars—Rowan; Fig. 3.1). No further structuring is normally needed in such cases.

In general terms, these descriptions of the methods used match Ericsson's principles, which are themselves quite general, though the detailed method differs with the task and the practitioner. In all cases the following procedures are apparent.

1. Part of the input is selected, such as a sequence of digits, a feature of a face, a nonsense syllable.
2. A verbal or visual associate to this part is retrieved (e.g. "a good mile time" or the word "teacher" in connection with the digit sequence, an image of oars or the word "oars" in association with large ears, a word sounding like the nonsense syllable, or a visual image corresponding to this word).
3. This is linked to other information as required (e.g. to the corresponding representation of the preceding item or a pre-learned structure or an associate which has to be learned). This step covers

Fig. 3.1. Example of a mnemonic for learning names to faces.

a multitude of possibilities, including labelling a digit sequence as "the second group" (SF), linking "teacher" with "mailbox" by imagery and both to a canteen to retain the line number (TE), placing an image at a location in Gorky Street (S), or linking "oars" to "Rowan" (name-learning mnemonic).

Ericsson's principles are thus too general and contain insufficient detail to provide an adequate account of the complexity of processes that are especially crucial in mastering a large quantity of information. He completely ignores the role of imagery, which SF appears not to have employed at all. However, most of the other cases described (though not VP) and those we have ourselves subsequently tested make extensive use of imagery for storing information.

MEMORY—ONE SYSTEM OR MANY?

While it may be reasonable to argue that specific memory abilities vary naturally between individuals, so that natural superiority may occur, it is more difficult to argue for a general variation in memory ability that will exhibit itself over a wide range of tasks (for example, as shown by Aitken). Current views favour a modular structure for memory, with separate specific systems handling different types of material or different types of storage. Clearly, if there is no single underlying memory system, correlated variation in efficiency across a wide range of tasks is unlikely. The evidence for the modular models of memory must now therefore be considered.

Typologies of Long-term Memory

Much current thinking about memory favours a multiple systems approach. Information is thought to be represented in a variety of different ways and retained in different functional brain systems, which may, but need not, be physically separated. Such a view should induce caution about the possibility of general memory superiority, as there is no common system on which it could depend, though there might be common characteristics of the different subsystems. Obviously specific superiority may depend on the operation of one or more of the specific systems.

The oldest suggested distinction within memory is that between short-term and long-term memory. In the currently most plausible analysis of the former, Baddeley and Hitch's (1974) Working Memory System (see also Baddeley, 1986), short-term memory is further subdivided into several interacting but distinct subsystems. Several researchers have investigated individual differences in the efficacy of these systems and their relation to performance on a variety of tasks. In the current context, however, it is long-term memory that is of primary interest. A number of dichotomous distinctions within long-term memory have been suggested by different researchers, the best known being those between episodic and semantic memory, between declarative and procedural memory, and between explicit and implicit memory. Schacter and Tulving (1994) conclude in a recent summary that at least five main systems can be distinguished in human memory: working (short-term) memory, semantic memory, episodic memory, procedural memory, and the perceptual representation system (see later).

None of the three dichotomous distinctions just referred to is completely clear-cut or acceptable. They are derived initially from differences associated with material or experimental procedure, rather than clear functional or neural independence. Episodic memory refers to memory for autobiographically experienced events, while semantic memory refers to factual information about the world. However, semantic memory must accrue through experience of specific events. A child might encounter a parrot for the first time and hear it sing the "Marseillaise". The child will remember this accomplishment as specific to this parrot unless parrots encountered subsequently also do the same, in which case it becomes known as a general feature of the breed. Thus, there is no difference in kind between these two possible types of memory record, only of generality of occurrence. This may then induce some different form of storage or affect the retrieval process. Declarative memory refers to the storage of factual information which can usually be expressed verbally, while procedural memory retains instructions for producing actions. However, most activities involve an amalgam of factual knowledge and actions (driving a car, for example, or playing a tune on the piano) and the distinction is heavily confounded with those between verbal and motor memory and between explicit and implicit memory.

Explicit and Implicit Memory

The distinction between explicit and implicit memory has generated a great deal of research in recent years and has produced the strongest grounds for the claim that there is not a single memory system. However, the relevance of this body of work to our current concerns is only marginal as all studies of superior memory performance have involved explicit memory tasks. Nevertheless, we will present a brief survey of the main issues, if only to indicate ways in which future investigation of superior memory may need to be expanded.

Explicit memory requires deliberate recall or recognition of material previously experienced, such as repeating a list of words, reproducing a movement or drawing a visual pattern. Implicit memory is shown indirectly by an effect of earlier experience on current behaviour, such as completion of word stems with words which have recently been seen rather than with equally plausible alternatives, or easier recognition of degraded drawings of objects that match drawings seen earlier, compared with recognition of similar drawings of objects not seen recently. Major research interest in this distinction has been provoked by the persistent finding that explicit memory may be destroyed in amnesic subjects while implicit memory is preserved. Several other differences between these two types of memory have also been demonstrated. Manipulation of depth of processing at the learning phase affects explicit but not implicit memory, while changes of physical features between the initial exposure and the test of the material, such as type face, do not affect explicit recognition but do affect implicit tasks. Also, items that are correctly recalled explicitly have only a chance probability of occurring in related implicit responses.

A prolonged debate has developed as to whether the observed dissociations between explicit and implicit tasks can be ascribed to differences in the storage systems involved or to differences in the type of processing within a single store (see Schacter, 1992). Some theorists argue that explicit recall depends on episodic memory, while implicit effects depend on a perceptual representation system (the PRS), itself possibly consisting of several subsystems. Demonstrations of conceptual priming in implicit tasks are explained as due to influences from the semantic memory system.

The main alternative to the multiple systems approach is the transfer-appropriate processing account, which argues that explicit and implicit memory tasks engage different processes. The version of this which has received most attention depends on the distinction between conceptually driven and data-driven processes. This view argues that both the encoding task and the recall task are normally conceptually driven in recall and therefore interact. For example, deeper processing engages conceptual processes and these are also involved in the explicit recall of a word list, while many tasks that test implicit memory, such as recognition of briefly presented words, are data driven, and hence are affected by physical features of the input.

While Blaxton (1989, 1992) did provide support for the importance of the distinction between conceptually driven and data-driven processing (rather than explicit and implicit memory), Cabeza and Ohta (1993) obtained dissociations which suggested that explicit memory, implicit conceptual memory, and implicit perceptual memory depended on different subsystems (which might be the episodic, semantic, and PRS systems respectively). A variety of other dissociations have been reported and claimed to match (more or less) distinctions broadly consonant with those listed by Schacter and Tulving (1994) and referred to earlier (e.g. Butters, 1989; Heindel, Butters, & Salmon, 1988; Keane, Gabrieli, Fennema, Gordon, & Corkin, 1991; Saint Cyr, Taylor, & Lang, 1988; Squire, Knowlton, & Musen, 1993; Tulving, Hayman, & Macdonald, 1991). Equally, however, dissociations have been reported that cast doubt on the validity of inferring separate memory systems for every pair of tasks which behave differently under some experimental variation (Ostergard, 1994; Perruchet & Baveux, 1989; Witherspoon & Moscovitch, 1989). Inferences of this type are logically suspect. If two tasks behave differently in response to some manipulation or neural damage, this implies that some process differs between the two tasks, hardly a surprising conclusion. It does not, however, follow that the tasks have nothing in common, either in the memory systems engaged, or in more basic underlying neural and biochemical processes. It is argued here, therefore, that none of the evidence for distinctions between explicit and implicit memory leads to the conclusion that no general memory factor or factors can exist.

Reber (1992) has discussed the distinction between explicit and implicit memory in detail in the context of a wide range of evidence indicating the importance of unconscious processes in human behaviour. He notes the various distinctions that have been drawn between different types of memory (p. 105) and concludes that, though the precise distinction being addressed is still as yet unclear, all these proposals probably reflect a single distinction, which he labels for convenience implicit vs. explicit memory and regards as one example of a broader underlying distinction between two types of psychological process. The first type is an evolution-arily older process not accessible to conscious awareness and relatively invulnerable to deterioration with age or brain damage (p. 118). The second type of process is open to voluntary control and introspection and is more sensitive to ageing and other neural impairments. The precise reasons for the differences in vulnerability are not discussed further, but differences in the complexity of the retrieval process are one possibility.

Some work by Ostergard (1994) is relevant and suggests an alternative approach to explaining the differences between explicit and implicit memory. He found that whether or not Alzheimer patients showed implicit priming effects depended on the nature of the retrieval cues provided. Episodic recall requires access to the elements associated with given temporal or spatial cues. Episodic recognition requires testing an element to see if it is associated with the appropriate temporal-spatial cues. Implicit tests depend on the probe's tendency to activate directly the same patterns in the nervous system as those activated during the priming phase. Hence, each of the test methods requires a different method of probing the memory system and a different direction for the spread of activation that evokes the response. These differences would be sufficient to explain dissociations between different explicit tests or between different implicit tests without postulating different subsystems.

Subdivisions within Explicit Memory

Studies of the effects of brain damage demonstrate a variety of specific defects within explicit memory, not all of which can unequivocally be categorised as defects of episodic or of semantic memory (see Hanley & Young, 1994, for a review). The findings demonstrate that sensory infor-mation from different modalities and of different types is analysed in different parts of the brain and the results of such analyses are retained as residual effects in the local analysing system (the PRS system or systems referred to earlier). For example, visual information about the structure of objects (or access to such information) may be lost (Beyn & Knyazeva, 1962; Davidoff & Wilson, 1985; Ratcliff & Newcombe, 1982). Zeki (personal communication) describes patients who were unable to see colours, remember the colours of objects, or dream in colour. Kapur, Heath, Meudell, and Kennedy (1986, see also De Renzi, Liotti, & Nichelli, 1987) describe a case where autobiographical events could be remembered but not famous faces, names, voices, or scenes from the past (unusually, new information could be retained). Levine, Warach, and Farah's (1985) patient was impaired on spatial memory but not on faces. In some cases information that can be retrieved by some routes is unavailable through others (Landis, Cummings, Benson, & Palmer, 1986; Pallis, 1955; Riddoch & Humphreys, 1987). Ability to retain a specific type of new information may be lost, while previously learned information of the same type is intact (Hanley, Pearson, & Young, 1990).

This picture of a variety of specific analysing systems is supported by studies of the effects of induced, rather than accidental, brain damage. Two major cortical perceptual and memory systems have been identified, the parvocellular system in the inferior temporal region of the visual cortex, which subserves object recognition, and the macrocellular system in the posterior parietal region, which is concerned with spatial position (Mishkin & Appenzeller, 1987; Ungeleider & Mishkin, 1982; see also Biederman et al., 1992, for related evidence drawn from human memory, and Tresch, Sinnamon, & Seamon, 1993, for a demonstration of selective interference with memory for spatial position or for shape).

Nadel and others (Nadel, 1994; O'Keefe & Nadel, 1978) have suggested two systems which integrate information from the specific systems, one of which (the locale system) achieves one-trial learning and preserves spatial information about single events, while the other (the taxon system) slowly constructs general, context-free representations (compare episodic and semantic memory).

These findings strongly suggest that highly specific memory subsystems exist, the efficiency of which may vary independently and lead to specific inferiorities and superiorities in memory performance. However, more general integrating processes are also necessary, the operation of which may be reflected in a range of different tasks. A variety of evidence indicates close interaction between supposedly different memory systems. Explicit recall of physical features is not impossible, though it is less efficient than recall of meaning. State-dependent effects on recall indicate that explicit recall can be affected by presumably implicit effects of physical features of the learning and recall situations. Effects of previously acquired semantic knowledge on explicit recall are also pervasive.

In conclusion, the evidence for a complex structural organisation of memory into specialist subsystems does not preclude overall variation in memory efficiency depending on common processes operating at a number of different levels. Strong evidence supporting such a common basis for many memory tasks comes from study of the amnesic syndrome.

The Amnesic Syndrome

In contrast to the evidence for specific systems handling information of a particular type, the amnesic syndrome provides evidence for a general loss of explicit memory over a wide range of material. The syndrome appears to represent a general impairment of either ability to encode memory in a form suitable for explicit retrieval or to retrieve encoded material explicitly, rather than a disorder of retention as such, since tests of implicit memory often demonstrate that material is present in memory. This is also supported by evidence that the rate of forgetting of material encoded into long-term memory by amnesics is no faster than it is in normals (Baddeley, 1990, p. 422).

The occurrence of amnesia of this kind implies that there is at least one major process that is common to memory for a large variety of types of material, since the amnesia may embrace memory for faces, names, routes, drawings, and episodes seen on television or described verbally. While immediate recall may be unimpaired, explicit recall after delays of more than a few minutes is impossible. Some theorists have also argued that different areas of brain damage produce different forms of the amnesic syndrome.

The most promising hypothesis concerning the nature of this impaired process is that advanced by Warrington and Weiskrantz (Weiskrantz, 1982), that it is the ability to organise material by linking new experiences together, including links to spatio-temporal context (see also Baddeley, 1990, p. 426). There is a marked similarity between this suggestion and the proposed functions of Nadel's locale system.

Distinguishing Impairments of Encoding, Storage, and Retrieval

Memory incorporates three main processes, encoding, retention, and retrieval, the efficiency of which may vary independently. Moss, Albert, Butters, and Payne (1986) have demonstrated that different types of disorder may produce differences in the nature of the amnesia. They found that Korsakoff patients demonstrated problems in initial registration of information (being particularly impaired by proactive interference and aided by opportunity to rehearse) but did not forget registered information any faster than a control group. Alzheimer patients, however, both encoded poorly and lost information rapidly over time. Patients with Huntington's disease showed much better performance in recognition, as opposed to recall, of verbal material (though recognition of other types of material was much worse than recognition of words). They also demonstrated variability in which words were recalled from trial to trial. Both findings suggest impaired retrieval. Obviously, if the three processes of encoding, retention, and retrieval can suffer independent impairment, they can contribute independently to superior performance.

Correlational Studies of Memory Abilities

The distinctions which have been drawn above between different memory systems depend on demonstrations that different memory tasks are differentially affected by specific variables such as depth of processing or by different types of brain damage, or by demonstrations that items eliciting correct responses in one type of task do not necessarily elicit correct responses in another type of task (dissociations).

Another approach to the problem of identifying differences in memory processes is through examination of correlations in performance over a range of tasks, and, when the data are adequate, through the technique of factor analysis. These procedures detect which types of task show correlated variation in performance over individuals and which types produce performances which vary independently across individuals. However, a demonstration that different groups of tasks can be identified that load differentially on different factors does not inevitably entail that these groups of tasks depend on distinct, physically separate memory systems. Differences may be due simply to differences in the processes required to encode or retrieve the information. For example, one group of tasks may require preservation of sequence while another group does not. Tasks that require preservation of sequence will tend to produce higher correlations in performance with each other than with tasks that make no such demand. Whether we wish to refer to an "order" memory system depends on the definition of "system" and our understanding of how memory functions. Higher order factors may also be derived on which the first-order factors load substantially, showing that all the tasks share a considerable amount of variance. Factor analysis is basically a descriptive procedure, the results of which depend heavily on the set of tasks and measures which are included and the analytic procedures adopted. These results require interpretation in terms of some theory about the structure of memory. Factor analysis is not a procedure which itself provides an unambiguous demonstration of the structure of memory. Studies employing this method have been restricted to explicit tasks and the data are, therefore, relevant solely to questions about the unity of episodic memory.

Carroll (1993) has recently examined all the available data within a comprehensive review of factor-analytic studies of cognitive abilities in general. He concludes (p. 302) that there is "a general memory ability that affects ... performances in a wide variety of tasks and behaviours involving memory" (p. 302). It is possible that there is also a separate general *learning* ability, reflected in variables such as rate of acquisition, as opposed to the abilities tested by a single exposure to the input, followed by recall or recognition after a short interval. This learning ability may be related to general intelligence. Carroll also identifies several specific memory factors that have been obtained consistently, and which are most typically represented in the following tasks: memory span, association learning, free recall, memory for meaningful material, and possibly memory for visual material. These factors emerged across a variety of different types of material.

It is noticeable that, while the neurophysiological and neuropsychological evidence isolates memory systems characterised by modality and type of input (e.g. colours, faces, verbal material, visual material—see Hanley & Young, 1994), the distinctions which emerge from the factorial studies are more closely related to the way the information is to be structured for retention, irrespective of the sensory modality through which it is presented. While neuropsychology identifies specific operations necessary to process and retain specific types of information, correlational analysis detects commonalities of operation in the intact processing system. Of the factors identified by Carroll, only the possible visual memory factor is characterised by sensory modality. Of the others, the meaningful memory factor (identification of which was somewhat speculative as the defining tasks varied between the different data sets) might be related to activity in semantic memory; both verbal and non-verbal tasks were found to load on it in different studies. The memory span factor might be related to components of Working Memory. However, association learning and free recall cannot be identified with any specific system that has emerged from neuropsychological evidence (no syndrome is characterised by loss of just one of these memory abilities), and it would seem that these two factors depend on the requirement for different types of operation within a single system (learning items plus links between them in the one case and learning only the items in the other). In addition to these specific factors, the factor analytic studies, like the studies of amnesics, indicate that there is a general memory factor common to a wide range of memory tasks.

Carroll notes that most of the correlational data come from studies employing a study phase and a test phase, which follows immediately, rather than studies employing extended learning procedures and/or testing after a delay. Only one study (Ingham, 1952) attempted a detailed study of retention and this study did identify a distinct *retention* ability, suggesting that efficiency of the storage phase may vary independently of other processes in memory (see also the work of Moss et al., 1986, discussed earlier, Rabbitt's findings described later in this chapter, and our own findings reported in Chapter 6).

Conclusions on the Separability of Memory Systems

Some of the neuropsychological evidence discussed previously demonstrates conclusively that different sorts of information require different parts of the brain for processing and storage. Either the ability to store new information or access to existing information may be lost, or both. However, it is probably misleading to depict these areas as dedicated memory "stores". In the recent past, the "store" metaphor (long-term store, short-term store, and so forth), supported by analogies drawn from the operation of computers, has tended to encourage a view of memory stores containing specific locations for each item. This store metaphor has been subjected to many attacks over the years, ranging from Lashley's (1929) failed search for the engram, through Restle's "Critique of Pure Memory" (1974) and Craik and Lockhart's (1972) advocacy of memories as by-products of perceptual and conceptual processing. Recently, Crowder (1993) has again argued for the greater plausibility of conceiving of memory as distributed residual activity following activation during sensory processing, or as a more lasting change in the nervous system due to such processing. Parallel Distributed Processing Models (see later) provide a plausible analysis of the way in which such processing systems may operate.

However, a system in which memory is fragmented, dispersed, and unconnected in this way would be of limited usefulness. Some method of integrating the different types of information is required. Rozin (1976) has suggested that, in the course of evolution, independent modular processing systems developed initially. Subsequently, in the interests of greater efficiency, these systems developed cross linkages to enable co-ordinated action. Hence, a more complex memory system has evolved to underpin more complex behaviour in more complex organisms. Both the occurrence of the general amnesic syndrome and the indications of a general memory factor from correlational studies support the possibility of a general memory system as well as specific subsystems.

Nadel's hypothesised "locale" system in the hippocampus appears to be operating in such a manner, combining the information from different sources into episodic memories for events occurring at specific temporal-spatial locations. In a similar vein, Grafman and Weingartner (1995) have proposed a Combinatorial Binding Model of memory. They suggest that there are two basic memory processes. Local cortical and subcortical operations retain unitised knowledge and features of incoming information. A second process binds together information from these different sources and is affected by hippocampal damage. Such binding together of information from diverse sources may involve previously associated items, or momentary linkage of hitherto unconnected items for a specific purpose. These integrating processes are also reminiscent of part of the role envisaged for the Central Executive of the Working Memory System. Whether an integrating system should be regarded as a "memory store", with its own set of duplicate memory traces, is as yet unclear (though not highly plausible) and is not vital for present purposes. Some single important episodes may also be retained more permanently; in the case of humans these form autobiographical memory, the establishment of which appears to depend on "refreshing" particular episodic memories (Nelson, 1993).

In addition to these relatively temporary episodic memories for single events, information must also be accumulated concerning regularities in the environment, as Nadel points out. These memories are "taxons" in Nadel's terminology, or semantic memory in the language of human memory research. It remains unclear whether or not these memories are stored again separately from the episodic memories from which they must be derived, though Nadel's argument that separation is necessary is persuasive.

The general failure of memory which is characteristic of the amnesic syndrome can most plausibly be ascribed, therefore, to failure in an integrative memory system. Though it was at one time argued that amnesia involved only episodic memory, leaving semantic memory intact, it has now been shown that this distinction is not tenable. Amnesics forget both general and specific newly acquired information, and have difficulty in retrieving older memories of both types. Implicit memories are intact, so it is the system or systems that co-ordinate and retrieve information in episodic memory (and also semantic memory) which are impaired in such subjects, and also in older subjects. Though there are obviously unanswered questions about the exact nature of this impairment, such a co-ordinating function would seem to require use of spatio-temporal information to tie together information derived from a single event. Amnesics commonly show "source forgetting" even when they can recall information to which they were exposed earlier; they cannot link this information to a specific spatio-temporal context in which it occurred. This suggests a breakdown of the co-ordinating system.

In the light of this argument, general superiority in memory is not incompatible with the existence of different memory subsystems and could be due to a number of factors: general properties of the nervous system affecting all the subsidiary memories from which episodic memory is constructed (see the later discussion of Parallel Distributed Processing Models), various aspects of the efficiency of the integrating system, and also of the system for retrieving information. The general properties of the nervous system should also affect implicit memory as well as explicit but there is as yet no evidence on relations between overall performance in the two types of task. The observed dissociation between responses to individual items in explicit and implicit memory does not necessarily entail that the overall levels of explicit and implicit performance will be unrelated across individuals. However, possible correlations between explicit and implicit performance will be obscured both by the operation of the co-ordinating system in the former case and the variation across individuals in the availability and efficiency of metacognitive processes employed in explicit retrieval.

Experimental studies on individual differences in memory efficiency, whether of large groups of the general population (see previously) or selected individuals with superior ability (see later), have employed batteries of episodic memory tasks. The evidence discussed previously shows that studies of the general population have tended to provide rather weak evidence for a general memory factor. There are likely to be a number of reasons for this. Variation in the tasks used will inevitably engage a variety of memory processes such as have been identified here and differences in these may often obscure more general features of performance. Also, most of the studies have concentrated on tasks involving a single presentation of the material, followed by a memory test after a fairly short interval. Memory in such paradigms is heavily dependent on efficiency in encoding and retrieval methods, which will frequently be task specific (depending on experience, learned techniques, motivation, etc.). Such specificity will further obscure any underlying general ability. Retention over a substantial interval has rarely been tested, though it may well be more revealing of individual differences in basic neural efficiency; Ingham's (1952) study, which made a detailed study of retention, found suggestive evidence for a distinct retention ability. Also, individual differences in retrieval ability have not been separated out from other aspects of memory. Finally, differences in general ability may only emerge clearly when exceptional individuals are studied.

Theoretical Models and Biological Facts

The recent revitalisation of Parallel Distributed Processing (PDP) or Connectionist models has provided a plausible demonstration of how processing and hence memory can be widely distributed yet retain specific information. Input is filtered through a massively parallel network of units, which are interconnected in a complex pattern. Connections between units are strengthened when the final output of the network is correct (in the sense of matching some desired outcome). Such systems are defined by the pattern of interconnections, the thresholds for the firing of the units, the rate of change in threshold strength, and the rate of decay of excitation. These parameters could vary across different processing subsystems or be subject to general genetic and environmental influences (such as diet, for example). Thus, this type of model leaves open the possibility of some overall consistency across subsystems in the efficiency of a whole variety of memory processes, which might produce overall variation in efficiency between individuals.

These models do not, however, offer any clear method of representing the role of special memory techniques. PDP models help us to conceptualise the internal working of processing modules, but more developed cognitive processes may have arisen through the development of a system for co-ordinating activity of these modules, as suggested previously. Most of the explicit memory tasks used by experimenters require retrieval of complex information from a specific spatio-temporal "window" and must engage these co-ordinating systems. They involve, therefore, an additional source of individual differences in overall memory efficiency, in addition to any variations in neural efficiency.

The neurobiological evidence indicates that even simple learning implicates a complex chain of events in the nervous system and that all these models are far too simple to reflect what happens in detail. Rose (1993, p. 271) argues that the formation of a representation in a chick's brain of an association between pecking a bead and a bitter taste, which will produce a lasting change in the chick's behaviour (refusing to peck the bead in future), requires a biochemical cascade of events in a localised region of the forebrain. This results in structural modifications to synapses and dendrites and is reflected in alterations in the electrical properties of the cells, shown by changes in their spontaneous activity in the hours after the experience. Rose (p. 313) offers the following summary of what he believes has been established:

> When an animal learns—that is, when it confronts some novel environment, some new experience which requires it to change its behaviour so as to achieve some goal—specific cells in its central nervous system change their properties. These changes can be measured morphologically, in terms of persistent modifications to the structure of the neurons and their synaptic connections as observed in the light or electron microscope. They can be measured dynamically, in terms of localized, transient changes in blood flow and oxygen uptake by the neurons during the processes of learning or of recall. They can be measured biochemically, in terms of a cellular cascade of

processes which begins with the opening of ion channels in the synaptic membranes and proceeds by way of coupled intracellular signals to the synthesis of new proteins which, inserted into the synaptic and dendritic membranes, are responsible for these morphological changes. And they can be measured physiologically, in terms of the changed electrical properties of the neurons that also result from their altered membrane structures.

Clearly, variation in the efficiency of retention in information will depend on the combined efficiency of a large number of different processes, which may depend on either general or localised properties of brain tissue.

RELATIONS BETWEEN MEMORY AND OTHER PSYCHOLOGICAL CONSTRUCTS

How, then, might such properties, and therefore memory efficiency, relate to other cognitive abilities? Is memory ability just one aspect of general intelligence? Is superior memory ability associated with vividness or other aspects of imagery, with consequences for thought processes? These were the last questions posed in Chapter 1. Little of the evidence described in Chapter 2 bears on them, but a variety of other research on memory is relevant and will now be considered.

Memory and Intelligence

It is commonly assumed that intelligent people learn more quickly. Since measured IQ is predictive of academic (and other) performance and a good memory is generally assumed to be necessary for such performance, it seems plausible that there should be a close relationship between measured IQ and memory ability. However, as Carroll (1993, p. 248) points out, "for various reasons it has been difficult to demonstrate this relation convincingly". Alternatively, memory and IQ may contribute independently to performance.

Relations between expertise in special fields (especially chess) and memory for information relevant to each field has been explored in some detail and the importance highlighted of large knowledge data bases and rapid access to such knowledge in the exercise of expertise. The prevailing view has been that improved memory for relevant material develops as a consequence of continued and frequent exposure, together with organisation of relevant knowledge, rather than being dependent on pre-existing superiority in the efficiency of memory processes (e.g. Ericsson & Faivre, 1988). However, there is usually no detailed evidence available on the memory ability of such experts prior to their involvement in their chosen field or on their memory ability in other areas. Gary Kasparov, the World Chess Champion, in reply to a question on BBC television shortly before the defence of his title in 1993, implied that natural memory ability was important for chess. Asked what was the single most important feature of the ability of a top chess player, he said, "An extraordinarily powerful memory and the ability to recall all known precedents in the opening, the middle game and especially the end game."

The issue of what, if any, relation exists between intelligence and memory ability is a complex one, to which relatively little research attention has been given. One obvious problem is the multifarious nature of memory. Another is the different demands made by IQ tests and memory tasks. The former are designed to eliminate effects of existing knowledge, thus excluding one possible influence of memory efficiency. Their main object is to detect ability to manipulate information, perceive relations, and extract rules. Their main demands are on short-term storage and working memory efficiency in speeded performance. It is not, therefore, surprising that recent investigations have concentrated on this aspect of memory function and that the only memory tests regularly included in IQ batteries involve tasks making this kind of demand.

In recent years there have been several studies examining relations between the functioning of Working Memory and other cognitive abilities. Daneman and Carpenter (1980) found correlations between their measure of Working Memory and both reading comprehension and the verbal Scholastic Aptitude Test (SAT). This measure requires a series of sentences to be studied and later the last word of each sentence has to be recalled. Carpenter, Just, and Shell (1990) have analysed the requirements of Raven's Matrices problems and argued, on the basis of somewhat indirect evidence, that performance on the test is related to ability to generate and maintain goals in Working Memory. Kyllonen and Christal (1990), in a study embracing over 2000 subjects, found high correlations between reasoning ability (assessed by a wide variety of psychometric tests) and Working Memory capacity, but also some evidence for independence of these two constructs, in that the former was correlated with general knowledge rather than speed of processing while the reverse was true for the latter. They suggest (p. 427) that "reasoning (or general ability) reflects working-memory capacity". Jurden (1995), however, found that verbal working memory performance was correlated with verbal IQ and computational working memory measures with non-verbal IQ. He also reanalysed the results of Kyllonen and Christal and showed that a more sophisticated analysis revealed a similar pattern in their data to that in his own study.

Relations between short-term memory ability and general ability have also been explored. A relation between IQ and memory span, especially backwards span, was found by Jensen and Figueroa (1975) and Hawkins and Kaye, cited in Mackintosh (1986). The latter found that backward span correlated with Daneman and Carpenter's measure of Working Memory. Cantor, Engle, and Hamilton (1991) found that both short-term memory span tasks and more complex measures of Working Memory capacity were positively correlated with performance on the verbal SAT. Furthermore, these relations were stronger when rehearsal was prevented, suggesting that use of simple strategies to aid memory can conceal basic memory capacities that are related to general intelligence (note also that backward span shows clearer relations to IQ than forward span). Cohen and Sandberg (1977), testing running memory span for digits, found that performance on the final digits was related to IQ score and suggested that individual differences in decay rate may be the critical attribute. This conclusion is at odds with a suggestion made by Dempster (1985), who tested recall of sentences presented twice, followed by a 15-second delay occupied with backward counting. He found that susceptibility to proactive inhibition (produced by presenting three similar sentences in succession) was negatively related to performance on the American College Test (a test of general ability, similar to the SAT, but simpler) and suggested that this could be due either to individual differences in the fineness of discrimination in the concepts activated by each sentence or the persistence of interference due to earlier sentences. Rapid decay would therefore be associated with superior performance, whereas Cohen and Sandberg (1977) suggested that slower decay might be associated with better performance. There were of course several differences in methodology that might produce a difference in result, but nevertheless there is clearly considerable scope for clarification in this area of research.

Mukunda and Hall (1992) carried out a meta-analysis of studies of the relation between recall of order and standardised achievement and aptitude tasks and found a consistent relation, especially when a distractor task was employed in addition to the recall of order; presumably such distractor tasks would also reduce the possibility of rehearsal or other strategies, so this result reinforces the suggestion of Cantor et al. (1991) above that basic memory ability, uncontaminated by metacognitive strategies, may show the clearest relation to other aptitudes. Miller and Vernon (1992) also found that a factor formed from a battery of short-term memory tasks was correlated with Spearman's g. They also claimed that a reaction time factor independently predicted g, but all the reaction-time tasks included a large memory component, so the validity of this claim is doubtful (see also Schweizer, 1993).

Hunt and his colleagues have conducted extensive investigations of relations between performance on psychometric tests and experimental cognitive tasks. Hunt, Lunneborg, and Lewis (1975) found that high scorers on verbal ability showed faster encoding and better short-term memory, while high scorers on quantitative ability showed resistance to interference and lower sensitivity to distraction. On long-term memory for word–digit pairs verbal ability was the best predictor of acquisition, but quantitative ability was the best predictor of recall after five weeks. Hunt (1980) comments that overall the correlations between information processing tasks and psychometric measures are moderate and only become large when extreme groups are considered.

Relations between intelligence and longer-term memory performance, which reflects organisation and retention rather than simply speed of encoding, are much less apparent than those between short-term memory measures and IQ. The general consensus is that long-term memory and IQ depend on different processes. Though some unified theories of cognition depend heavily on memory processes (Anderson, 1983; Newell, 1990), a recent comprehensive theory of intelligence (Anderson, 1992) does not include any distinct memory component, so there is no scope in the theory for variation in individual memory ability. The genetic component in memory appears to be low compared with that in IQ (Finkel, Pedersen, and McGue, 1993; Plomin, 1988). Idiots-savants may display unusual memory ability along with low measured IQ. Studies of relations between measured IQ and performance on a variety of other memory tasks have not produced evidence for strong links between the two (e.g. Powers, Andriks, & Loftus, 1979, looking at relations between intelligence and eyewitness accuracy; Rule & Jarrell, 1983, who obtained modest correlations between IQ and age of earliest memory).

There are a number of possible reasons for the observed lack of association which should be considered before concluding that the case is proven that IQ measures and memory performance reflect different underlying abilities. First, it may be argued that, if we are concerned with the contribution of memory to general cognitive performance, it is not IQ measures that should be considered but performance in real-world situations. As has been frequently observed, high IQ score is only a moderate predictor of such performance and sometimes a poor one. The classic study on this issue is that of Ceci and Liker (1986) who found that individuals who scored well below average on formal IQ tests were successfully manipulating a sophisticated system, involving a large number of interacting variables, in calculating handicapping rates on the horse racing track. In cases of expertise such as these a strong relation is commonly observed between degree of expertise and memory for relevant material, but this is probably because expertise aids memory rather than vice versa. Accordingly, no clear answer concerning relations between memory and intelligence is likely to emerge from studies of this kind.

Second, in general only limited aspects of memory performance have been investigated when evaluating relations between memory and IQ. Studies have concentrated on tasks involving a study phase followed by a test phase after only a short interval. Carroll (1993, p. 284) points out that, because exposure times in the study phase are normally controlled, these tasks in effect measure learning speed rather than retention over a substantial interval (obviously a study requiring learning to criterion over a series of trials distributed over time incorporates both these processes). In the light of the previous discussion and other evidence discussed later (e.g. Anderson, 1992), such a speed factor may also be involved in the measurement of IQ. However, other factors may negate this relation. Speed of learning may not depend on the same processes as speed of manipulating information in Working Memory. Also additional processes of retention and retrieval are involved in the memory tasks. The suggestion that processing speed is a general parameter of the individual central nervous system which underlies all cognitive performance will be discussed later.

Carroll also points out that there are few studies that focus on the relation between learning rate and rate of forgetting which occurs after the learning phase, or of individual differences in these relations. It is possible that it is retention that is related to IQ rather than the efficiency of the learning or encoding phase, which will affect mainly immediate memory performance. The available evidence on these issues is varied. Carroll (1993, p. 302) concludes that:

> there is a general learning ability that is positively and substantially correlated with performance that is loaded with broad second-order factors of cognitive ability, particularly fluid and crystallised intelligence. It is possible that there is a component of general learning ability that is not predicted by cognitive ability tests, but no persuasive evidence for such a component exists in the available literature.

Stake (1961) calculated parameters of learning curves on a number of tasks and found that the rate of learning and the asymptote of the learning curve were related to scholastic aptitude (correlations ranged from +0.10 to +0.60). Stake concluded that "the findings of this study revealed no general learning ability other than the general aptitude that is measured by such tests as an intelligence test given just once" (p. 44). This seems somewhat over optimistic, given the modest size of the obtained correlations. Carroll (1993) reanalysed Stake's data and, while obtaining rather a different factor structure, concluded (p. 288) that "the study as a whole tends to support Stake's conclusion that intelligence (i.e., cognitive ability) is related to ability to learn, and that there is no important learning ability factor that is independent of intelligence" (p. 288). Ingham's (1952) study, referred to earlier, extracted a general retention factor, but it was less strongly related to Spearman's g than were the learning phase and immediate recall (g contributed 20.1% to the variance of the former and 32.6% to the latter); this study, therefore, is consistent with Stake's result. Dube (1977) also found that more able subjects showed better memory for a story, but this could have reflected better comprehension rather than simply memory ability.

Several other studies fail to support these relations. A study by Allison (1960) found that learning rate was partly independent of general ability. Klausmeier and Feldhusen (1959) found no significant differences associated with intelligence in retention over six weeks of arithmetical counting and addition skills. Haywood and Heal (1968) found no significant association between IQ level in learning-disabled groups and acquisition or retention of associations between visual patterns. Within each IQ level individuals who showed rapid acquisition also showed less forgetting, suggesting a memory ability separate from IQ.

Reber (1992) makes some interesting but speculative suggestions which need to be tested. He argues that the efficiency of implicit processes varies less across individuals than the efficiency of explicit processes, and that such variation as exists in implicit processes is less closely related than variation in explicit processes to formal measures of IQ. He suggests, however, that efficiency of implicit processes may be more closely related than efficiency of explicit processes to "intelligence" (as opposed to formal IQ measures). By "intelligence" Reber intended to refer to ability to cope with real-life tasks, such as was demonstrated in the study of calculating handicaps in horse racing by Ceci and Liker (1986) referred to earlier. Reber, Walkenfeld, and Hernstadt (1991) obtained supporting evidence but McGeorge, Crawford, and Kelly (in press), while confirming the pattern of results obtained, suggested that the correlation of implicit memory measures with measures of intelligence was low because the measures of implicit memory were of low reliability and uncontrolled for age; also, only summary IQ measures were employed. A more detailed analysis showed that neither explicit nor implicit memory was significantly related to a verbal ability factor (linked to crystallised intelligence), but both tasks had significant loadings on a Perceptual Organisation factor (linked to fluid intelligence). Furthermore, explicit and implicit memory had opposite loadings on an Attention–Concentration factor, the explicit task having a positive loading and the implicit task a negative one (though only the former reached a significant level). This study implies that relations between memory abilities and intelligence measures may be quite complex.

There is a growing consensus that speed of neural processing is strongly related to measured IQ (see, for example, Anderson, 1992) and it has also been suggested that the decline in cognitive functions, especially memory, with age is due to decreased speed of processing (e.g. Salthouse, 1985). It would also seem to imply that memory performance depends primarily on the efficiency of initial encoding. This could be superior in a faster system, for example, because it would permit richer encoding of the input and interconnections would develop more reliably between bursts of activity that are closely related temporally. The possibility that memory performance may also depend on retention and that retention may depend on other aspects of neural function is not given any prominence.

Relevant evidence on this issue has begun to emerge from detailed work on relations between age and cognitive functioning carried out by Rabbitt and his associates (for a summary see Rabbitt, 1993a or 1993b). Yang Qian and Rabbitt (see Rabbitt, 1993b, p. 424) equated initial recall from a word matrix by older and younger subjects by varying the exposure time, then delayed recall for varying intervals. Older subjects needed longer exposure to achieve the same level of immediate recall as younger subjects (i.e they demonstrated slower processing) and still showed more forgetting from the same baseline. The best fitting model indicated that age affected memory via its effects on both processing rate and forgetting rate and also indicated that these two effects on memory were independent. Thus, retention is not dependent simply on processing speed at the initial encoding.

In a further study (1993b, p. 426ff.), Rabbitt administered the Cattell Culture Fair IQ test, together with tests of information processing rate and memory, to 375 subjects aged 50 to 86. The dominant factor that was extracted accounted for 26% of the variance and included measures of processing rate and IQ but not age; a second factor, accounting for 24% of the variance included free recall, object recall, IQ, and age (see Table 3.1). Hence, memory differences were associated with age but not with differences in speed of processing, though IQ was related to both speed and memory ability. Age was associated more strongly with memory scores than with speed scores, contrary to the view of Salthouse (1985). Other related studies carried out by this group have produced a similar pattern, with age loading on a memory factor rather than on an IQ plus speed factor. The dissociation between IQ and memory increases with age because more individuals appear whose memory performance falls disproportionately below what would be expected on the basis of their IQ. Nettelbeck and Rabbitt (1992) found that partialling out measures of processing speed eliminated the relation between age and many measures of cognitive performance, but the relation between age and (mainly short-term) memory performance survived, again suggesting that some aspect of memory is related to factors other than processing speed.

These results demonstrate that processing speed is strongly related to many aspects of cognitive performance measured by IQ tests. Also, some aspects of memory performance are related to IQ, but this relation does

TABLE 3.1

Loadings of Memory and Cognitive Tests, IQ, and Age on
Factors Extracted from Rabbitt's (1993b) Study

	Factor 1	Factor 2
Free recall	0.15	0.93
Object recall	0.28	0.52
Letter substitution (coding)	0.82	0.19
Visual search	0.85	0.05
Cattell Culture Fair Test	0.58	0.56
Age	−0.21	−0.92

not depend on processing speed. Memory performance is only weakly related to processing speed and is related to IQ only insofar as some components of the latter are not due to processing speed. Retention is a possible candidate for the process which underpins memory efficiency and these aspects of general intellectual ability.

In conclusion, the weight of the evidence indicates that memory ability is not coterminous with general intelligence and that, in order to understand individual differences in general cognitive performance, both need to be considered and their relative contributions assessed.

Memory and Imagery

Overall relations between memory and imagery can be examined in a variety of tasks to discover in which conditions the occurrence of imagery is related to memory performance. Individual differences in imagery and in memory ability and possible relations between the two abilities are the main focus of interest in the present context. Are subjects who demonstrate superior memory performance possessed of superior imagery ability and vice versa?

There is a substantial body of evidence supporting a correlation between imageability, concreteness of material, and recall performance. For example, Sadoski and Quast (1990) found that the most memorable parts of articles recalled after a 16-day delay were significantly related to imagery ratings. Imaginal mediators have been widely shown to aid learning (Richardson et al., 1987), but Denis, Engelkamp, and Mohr (1991) found that, while visual imagery aided paired-associate learning of action verbs, motor-kinaesthetic imagery had the reverse effect.

Ernest (1977) reviewed the evidence for relations between individual imagery ability and memory and concluded that they depended both on the task and the measure of imagery employed. The measures can be self-report of vividness or control of imagery or objective tests of visuo-spatial processing. Vividness of imagery could be seen as one type of memory ability, though the evidence of Sheehan and Neisser (1969) does not support this, while control of imagery and visuo-spatial tasks involve other processes.

Ernest (1977) notes several studies reporting better incidental recall in subjects scoring high on all three measures, offering some support for a common underlying process mediating retention. Self-reported vividness of imagery was not, however, related to deliberate verbal learning, though the other measures were so related (in certain conditions), suggesting that, when controlled strategic processes are engaged, facility in these is more important than the underlying retention process (cf. Denis, 1987, who draws a similar conclusion). This conclusion is consonant with the findings that the positive relation between objective spatial ability measures and memory is restricted to situations in which the task encourages imagery or where use of imagery is difficult. McKelvie (1995) reached a similar conclusion. When verbal processing is encouraged, no relation or a negative relation occurs, especially in female subjects. This effect is explicable if subjects who are low in spatial ability tend to concentrate on verbal processing and hence can cope better when this mode of processing is required. MacLeod, Hunt, and Mathews (1978) showed that subjects adopt strategies appropriate to their skills, where different methods of carrying out a task are possible.

McKelvie (1995), in a later review, highlighted a number of task differences which moderate the relation between reported vividness of imagery and memory. Such a relation is not found for paired-associate learning unless individual differences are extreme or interacting pictures serve as stimuli, but is found in free recall, especially with concrete words and delayed testing. For recognition, no relation is normally found, though it may occur with material such as complex scenes and narrative text. Denis (1987) found that vivid imagers showed significantly higher retention of prose when instructed at encoding to generate visual images of the details described. Hanggi (1989) found that the superiority of vivid imagers in a visual short-term memory task was enhanced under conditions of articulatory suppression. Several researchers have demonstrated superior memory for colour in subjects with high imagery scores (see Richardson, 1994). Tanwar and Malhotra (1990, 1992a, 1992b) showed that high imagery ability, combined with instructions to use imagery, improved performance on several short-term memory tasks. Wilding, Rashid, Gilmore, and Valentine (1986) found that use of imagery induced by instructions was more beneficial for long-term than for short-term memory.

Hishitani (1985) demonstrated that connecting three nouns by imagery was more beneficial for immediate unexpected recall than relating them by a sentence. However, more forgetting occurred in the first case and both conditions produced equal recall a week later. Vivid imagers (indicated by self-report) performed better than poor imagers under sentence-generation but not image-generation conditions; this finding is at odds with McKelvie's conclusion mentioned previously and suggests that vivid imagers used imagery spontaneously. Vivid imagers also showed less forgetting in the imagery-generation condition than poor imagers. Hishitani suggests that image formation requires more input elaboration than sentence generation and this is more complex in vivid imagers, as shown by their image descriptions. However, the absence of any superiority after a week for image generation compared with sentence generation shows that instructions do not have the same effect as individual differences in vividness of imagery. This study further reinforces the absence of any simple relations between the measures and the need to take into account all aspects of the task as well as individual differences before drawing any conclusions.

These observations support the unsurprising conclusion that relations between reported visual imagery ability and memory performance are more apparent when the task lends itself to or encourages use of visual imagery.

An alternative approach to the issue is to examine the performance of criterion groups. Lindenberger, Kliegl, and Baltes (1992) found that graphic designers were superior to controls on a cued recall variant of the method of loci, and a review by Isaac and Marks (1994) concluded that introspective reports of imagery experience are systematically related to age, gender, and specialisation, consistent with the view that mental imagery plays a key role in planning and implementing action.

Two studies suggest some relation between imagery and access to early memories (Daniel, 1981; Richardson, 1994) with subjects who report more vivid imagery reporting more childhood memories.

Explanations for the effects of imagery on memory may lie in encoding and/or retrieval processes. Paivio (1971) postulated a dual-coding hypothesis and Rohwer (1970) postulated a semantic elaboration hypothesis. Marschark and Surian (1989) prefer an explanation in terms of inter-item relations and favour recall rather than encoding as the locus. Most of this evidence, which demonstrates the importance of the instructions and task in determining the relation between reported imagery and memory, supports the importance of processes operating at encoding.

In conclusion, superior visual imagery ability clearly aids memory performance when task demands facilitate its use. The issue of whether superior visual imagery is a necessary or sufficient condition for superior memory performance (at least in certain tasks) seems not to have been addressed in any study prior to those we shall be reporting later.

This chapter concludes our review of the theoretical background and empirical literature relevant to the questions posed about the nature and nurture of superior memory at the end of Chapter 1. In the next chapter we proceed to describe our own experimental investigations.

4 The Search for Superior Memories: Is Anyone Out There?

The study of TE described in Chapter 2 demonstrated that exceptional memory performance could be attained on a wide variety of tasks by applying a quite limited range of mnemonic methods in a flexible manner. Where direct comparison was possible, TE matched the performance of the classic cases of superior memory described in detail by Luria and by Hunt and Love and his explanations of his methods raised questions about the determinants of performance at this level. However, it was not clear whether such levels of performance must always depend on technique, whether a similar level could be demonstrated that depended on natural ability alone, or whether a combination of these two components was required. Nor did we know how many subjects might be found who were able to demonstrate performance at this level, or the feasibility of locating such individuals in the general population. A radio broadcast provided an opportunity to explore this issue by soliciting volunteers who believed themselves to have unusual memory ability, and we were able to select ten of these volunteers for further study, mainly on the basis of geographical convenience.

At this stage the goals of the proposed study were to find examples of claimed superior memory ability and discover how good the individual's memory ability was. However, this immediately raised other questions about the selection of tasks that would be needed to provide a satisfactory test. The studies of TE had used both some of the well-established tests of (mainly short-term) memory (the Brown–Peterson task, digit span, number matrix learning) and also some tasks resembling everyday demands on memory (story, faces, names). TE had demonstrated superior performance in both types of task. Would this be true in other cases or would memory ability often turn out to be specific to certain tasks, these varying between individuals? In support of their claims to superior memory, our volunteers were citing everyday memory abilities such as autobiographical memory and memory for factual information (though some also claimed specialist expertise such as memory for railway timetables). Should we therefore aim to test memory for a wide variety of *material* or employ a wide variety of memory *tasks* (digit span, paired-associate learning, etc.)? Theories of memory were not sufficiently explicit to enable identification of a set of tests which would target all the main hypothetical subtypes or subcomponents or distinct memory processes, and there was little conclusive evidence on the relations between tasks commonly used by psychologists and memory ability in everyday life.

A further factor to be taken into account was the nature of our subjects, who would have little or no experience of test situations and were in several cases quite elderly. It seemed desirable that the tasks to be employed should generally resemble everyday memory tasks and the procedures should be easy to explain and require minimal practice. Consequently, to the tasks employed in the second study of TE (story, faces, names) we added others to increase the range of materials and memory components: free recall of words, learning telephone numbers to names (to introduce numbers and also association learning), names of Prime Ministers since the Second World War (to test already existing memories), snow crystals (visual patterns) and the temporal sequence and spatial positions of a series of pictures (a simple form of event memory which is discussed further later). We also asked subjects to recount their earliest memory and we included an unexpected retest on four of the tasks a week later (story, faces, names, and word list).

Many aspects of memory were not covered. There was no systematic comparison of recall and recognition performance, which might have indicated to what extent any superiority was dependent on superiority in retrieval, as opposed to retention. Memory for real-life events (such as is required in eyewitness testimony), and for music and movements was not tested. And the tests were essentially all explicit, declarative, episodic memory tests, partly because the implicit/explicit distinction had not yet emerged as a prominent aspect of memory research and partly because it would be difficult, in the context of an overt investigation of memory ability, to include a task that could with confidence be regarded as exclusively implicit.

THE TASKS

A detailed description will now be given of the tests used in this first study. Tests added in later studies will be described when the appropriate study is introduced. In all the memory tasks subjects were informed before presentation of the material that their memory for it would be tested.

Story Recall

"The story of Maakga and Inkanyamba" was taken from Dube's study described in Neisser (1982). It was presented on tape in a male voice, read in a natural way and lasted for six minutes. The story is an African folktale with marked supernatural and symbolic elements. The same supernatural being is referred to under different embodiments at different times without explicit explanation, so considerable inference is needed to construct the theme. The sequence of events, recounted in considerable (and sometimes redundant) detail in the original, is readily telescoped, transmuted, and simplified without losing the main theme, so a wide range of performance is possible.

Subjects were required to retell the story orally after a single hearing, not necessarily in the exact words of the original, but including as much of it as they could remember. These accounts were transcribed and scored by two judges, using Dube's original division into 99 "themes", each given 2 points to yield a maximum possible score of 198. This enabled comparison with Dube's own results but did not prove entirely satisfactory because several themes contained more than one meaningful idea. Hence, a system of awarding half points as well as integers was employed. The scores given independently by the two judges were averaged if the differences were less than six points; otherwise differences on individual themes were discussed and rescored until agreement was achieved within the required limits. A further inadequacy of the marking scheme was that failure to preserve the original sequence was not penalised. Several events could be temporally interchanged without substantially affecting the overall sense of the story. This frequently happened but the subjects who retained the original sequence received no credit for doing so. No mention is made of this problem in Dube's account so we had to assume that a similar method of scoring for item occurrence without strict adherence to the original sequence was employed.

Subjects were further required to retell the story a week later. Wherever possible, this was done at a second test session incorporating all the delayed memory tests and some of the other tasks also.

Sometimes this was impossible due to geographical distance or other constraints; subjects in such cases were sent a blank tape and asked either to retell the story orally or to write down their version if this was not possible.

This task was chosen as a test of memory for a meaningful series of events, resembling a common use of memory to encode, retain, and recount information acquired verbally from others. It clearly requires a complex integration of linguistic and cognitive abilities involved in comprehending and organising the content, not just pure memory.

Face Recognition

For this task 36 photographs of faces (18 male and 18 female) were shown for five seconds each. Then after an interval of two to three minutes, during which subjects recounted their earliest memory, the same photographs were shown in the same order, each paired with another which had not been seen before (pairs were selected to be similar in appearance; Fig. 4.1). The previously seen face appeared randomly on the left or the right. Subjects had to indicate whether the previously seen photo was on the left or the right. The number of correct choices was calculated.

For the delayed test the same pairs of photographs were shown again in the same order, with the positions re-randomised, and responses were made as before. Again, this test was carried out as far as possible in a second test session, but some subjects were sent photocopied sheets with the pairs of photographs on them and asked to tick them in exactly the same way. These same photocopies were also used when the test was made during a second test session.

Fig. 4.1. Examples of forced-choice face recognition task; in each pair one face is new and one has been seen before.

This task was chosen as representing a common demand upon everyday memory. However, in the light of work carried out over the past 10 years, it was clearly not a true test of *face* recognition but rather one of picture recognition, since the same photos were used in all three presentations, rather than pictures with different poses or expressions being introduced.

A second weakness was the use of the same foils in both the immediate and the delayed recognition tests. Delayed recognition therefore became a test of distinguishing photos which had been seen once (that is, the foils seen in the immediate recognition test) from those which had been seen twice (the targets). The procedure may have induced repetition of errors but arguably the main effect would be to make the task more difficult than it would have been if a new set of foils had been used, rather than tapping a completely different ability.

The main problem of this task, which was taken from McKelvie (1978), was that it proved too easy. Several of the control group (see later), as well as subjects with superior memory ability, achieved a perfect score on the immediate recognition test, so it did not enable unusually high levels of performance to be adequately assessed.

Learning Names to Faces

This task was based on one used by Morris, Jones, and Hampson (1978). Thirteen photographs of female faces (different from those used in the previous task) were shown, with a surname, for 10 seconds each. The order was then rearranged (in the same way for all subjects) producing a delay of one to two minutes, and the photos were shown again without the names for up to 10 seconds each. Subjects had to write down the name they believed had been associated with each face, or leave a blank. Delayed recall followed the same pattern, with the faces in a different order. This was again carried out in the second session or by post, using photocopies in the same way as for the face recognition test above. Minor misspellings were disregarded in the scoring and the number of names correctly given was recorded.

This task was chosen to mimic another common memory demand. It proved to be a very difficult task for most subjects, particularly the delayed recall.

Free Recall of Words

Twenty-five common words were shown for one second each, with a two-second pause between items. Subjects were then asked immediately to write down all the words they could recall in any order. A week later they carried out a further recall in a second session or by postal request.

The number of items recalled was checked and also the number of false alarms (intrusions).

This task was employed as a standard memory task, the properties of which are well known. It does not correspond closely with any everyday memory task (apart, possibly, from remembering a shopping list). The set of words and norms was taken from Mohindra (1983).

Learning Name–number Pairs (Telephone Numbers)

Six surnames, each with a six-digit "telephone number", were shown in succession for 10 seconds each. The names were then presented in random order on a sheet of paper and subjects were asked to supply the telephone numbers. This procedure was carried out twice more and the number of digits recalled in the correct position on the third run (maximum possible 36) was recorded. A few subjects in later studies scored the maximum on the first run. Delayed testing was attempted but hardly any subjects could recall even a single digit, so the delayed task was only offered optionally to memory experts once this became apparent.

This task was devised especially for the study, being equivalent to a common everyday memory requirement (though in an extreme form). It also included the only requirement to learn numbers in the study, but it did of course also require associations to the correct name to be retained and in this respect it resembled the commonly used paired-associate learning task.

Recalling Names of British Prime Ministers Since the Second World War

This test was included in an attempt to include a test of memory for some commonly available general knowledge. In the U.S.A., recall of American Presidents is commonly used for this purpose, but since all children are exposed to this list at school it can be assumed that approximately equal opportunity has been given to learn the information in all cases. No obvious equivalent is apparent for British children, though Warren and Groom (1984) have used recall of British Prime Ministers since the First World War. The task selected here was intended to be a simpler one, but it soon became apparent that performance depended heavily on age, with older people doing better as they had directly experienced the events associated with each name. Interests also played a major role. Hence, results from this task presented a very different picture from most of the others and the task was not primarily a test of memory in the same sense as the others were.

Recall of Spatial and Temporal Location of a Sequence of Pictures

Eight pictures of common objects were presented one at a time for one second each. Each picture appeared randomly in one of eight locations in a left to right array, the temporal order in which pictures occurred at these locations being random (Fig. 4.2). Thus, the first picture might appear at the sixth location from the left, the next at the first position and so on. After all eight pictures had been presented they were shuffled and subjects were asked to place them either in the spatial locations at which they had appeared or in the temporal sequence in which they had been shown. Subjects did not know beforehand which attribute would be tested. In two initial practice trials they were told beforehand in order to get them used to the task; they then had two further practice trials in which they were not informed until after presentation of the pictures. Four test trials were given, two for the temporal condition and two for the spatial condition, in random order. Subjects did not know how many test trials were to be given, so could not reliably predict which attribute would be tested on each trial. The number of correctly placed pictures was counted, an average calculated for each attribute, and these averages were summed to give a total score.

This task was taken from Anderson (1976) and was intended as a test of ability to retain spatial and temporal attributes of items. Some theorists (e.g. Hasher and Zacks, 1979) have claimed that these attributes are processed automatically; if this is correct the task tests a different type of memory ability from those that require cognitive processing or that benefit from rehearsal. Only later did we appreciate a less debatable and potentially more important attribute of the task, that it was very difficult to apply preorganised practised strategies to solve it, so it tested primarily automatic or natural memory.

Recognition of Snow Crystals

This task was adopted from Goldstein and Chance (1970) and was included as a test of memory for visual patterns which could not readily be encoded precisely in verbal form.

Fourteen pictures of snow crystals were shown for three seconds each with seven seconds between each presentation (Fig. 4.3). They were then shown again mixed in with 70 foils. Subjects were required to tick on a list whether each of these 84 patterns had been seen before or not. Following the procedure of the original experiment, subjects were informed that they should keep their positive identifications to about 14

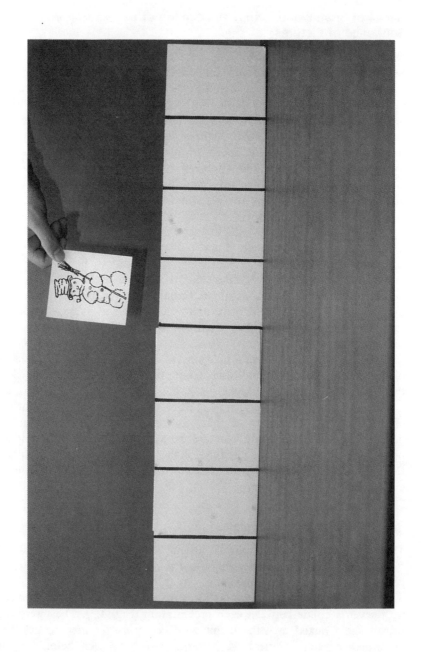

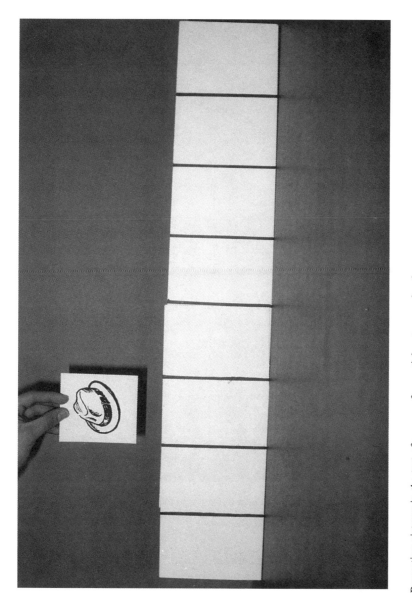

Fig. 4.2. Presenting pictures in the test of memory for spatial or temporal order.

Fig. 4.3.   Examples of snow crystals used in the test of memory for a visual stimulus.

in number. The original experimenters reported that their subjects were able to do this without any major problem, but many of our subjects found it difficult to follow this instruction, since they had no idea at the beginning of the test stimuli how the targets would be distributed in the sequence or of the degree of similarity between targets and foils. Hence, it was difficult for them to settle on an appropriate level of confidence for making a positive identification.

Goldstein and Chance used the number of hits as their measure of performance, which would be satisfactory if all subjects employed the same response criterion (i.e. made exactly 14 positive identifications) but was highly unsatisfactory if the number of positive responses varied between subjects. Consequently, in the present studies the Signal Detection parameter d' was employed, which is a criterion-free measure of discrimination between targets and foils.

This task was also not readily amenable to any special memory technique, partly due to the unfamiliar nature of the material, but also due to subjects' ignorance about the precise nature of the test situation to be employed. Several of the more expert subjects tested in later studies indicated that they would have been able to devise suitable methods of improving performance greatly if they had been required to tackle the task a second time, by focusing on specific attributes of the targets and using verbal encodings to retain them.

THE CONTROL GROUP

Initially, norms for these tasks were taken from the original studies on which the tasks were based. Subsequently, data were collected from a control group for all the tasks. This group covered a wide age range to match that of the experimental subjects (35 to 75 years in the initial study). The control subjects were obtained from a variety of sources: technical, secretarial, and academic staff at Royal Holloway college in London, mature students in their first term studying psychology, a subject panel collected for a study of driving behaviour, a club for the elderly, and personal contacts. Some of the subjects were in their 70s and 80s, but these were not included in the calculations of norms as it was apparent that performance on most tasks declined at an accelerated rate in subjects over the age of 70. Consequently, norms were calculated from 31 subjects (8 male and 23 female) aged between 30 and 70, using multiple regression to calculate expected values on each task at any given age. Some experimental subjects in later studies were aged less than 30, but these were compared against norms for 30-year-olds, rather than attempting to project results to ages below the minimum of the control group. It seemed unjustified to assume that age effects up to the age of 30 would be parallel to those over the 30 to 70 range and it was clear that projections below 30 years produced implausibly high estimates of performance for subjects in their 20s (for example, predicting that subjects of undergraduate age would consistently achieve perfect performance on the face recognition task and near perfect performance in the free recall of 25 words). Means calculated for each test for 30-year-olds, the regression coefficients for age,

TABLE 4.1

Mean Scores for a 30-year-old Subject, Together with Range of Obtained Scores,
Standard Errors, and Regression Coefficients for Age and Mill Hill Score

	Mean	Range	SD	β (Age)	β (Mill Hill)	Maximum Possible
Story						
immediate	65	31–114	27.3	−0.30	0.50*	198
delayed	54	0–95	28.6	−0.70*	0.38	198
Faces						
immediate	35.8	26–36	3.2	−0.09*	−0.05	36
delayed	29.0	18–33	3.7	−0.19**	0.02	36
Names						
immediate	3.7	0–10	2.7	−0.04	0.02	13
delayed	1.4	0–4	1.4	−0.04*	0.00	13
Words						
immediate						
correct	16.25	5–20	3.2	−0.19**	0.01	25
intrusions	1.60	0–4	1.2	0.00	−0.01	–
delayed						
correct	9.50	0–14	2.5	−0.23**	−0.03	25
intrusions	3.80	0–10	2.6	0.02	−0.06	–
Telephone numbers						
immediate	16	2–30	7.3	−0.24*	0.07	36
delayed	0	–	–	–	–	36
Prime Ministers						
correct	5.11	4–9	1.4	0.03	0.04**	9[1]
intrusions	0.03	0–1	0.4	0.00	0.01	–
Pictures						
combined	10.7	5–14	2.3	−0.05	−0.01	16
Snow crystals						
d′	0.87	0.19–1.73	0.48	−0.01	0.01	–
Beta	2.22	1.01–10.81	1.8	−0.05	0.02	–
Age of earliest memory	3.39	1.30–14.00	2.4	0.07	−0.04	–
Mill Hill percentile	83.0	47.00–100.00	15.2	–	–	100

These estimates of the standard deviations are corrected for the difference between the obtained mean Mill Hill score of the group and a mean at the 50th percentile. Including this correction slightly increases the estimates and changes some estimates of individual differences from the control mean in subsequent tables, compared with previously published data (Wilding & Valentine, 1994b). *$P < .05$; **$P < .01$ (one-tailed tests in all cases).

[1]When the task was first used, there were nine eligible Prime Ministers. The later addition of John Major has been ignored for scoring purposes.

and for the percentile achieved on the Mill Hill vocabulary scale (Test B: synonyms) are shown in Table 4.1.

Performance by individuals will normally be expressed as a z score in relation to the predicted score for an individual of the same age, calculated by regressing scores in the control group on age. Immediate recognition of faces produced many scores close to ceiling and delayed recall of names to faces produced many scores of zero. Consequently, performance on these tasks was not strictly suitable for regression analysis. Nevertheless, results of the analyses have been reported in order to provide a complete picture. In later studies, Mill Hill vocabulary score was also entered into the regression equation and the predicted score adjusted to match the Mill Hill score of the subject under discussion. Since no Mill Hill scores were taken in the earlier studies, predicted scores are for a Mill Hill score at the 50th percentile (i.e. average ability). In calculating the z score for each individual in these circumstances the standard error of the regression line has to be corrected for the distance of the individual's score on the independent variable from the control group mean (the standard error increases as age or Mill Hill score departs further from the mean of the control sample). The method of carrying out this correction is given in the Appendix at the end of this book.

When examining retention over a week, percentage retained will be given as the raw score. The contributions of age, Mill Hill score and initial performance to retention were tested as follows. It was first established that the Mill Hill score had no significant or substantial effect on any of the four retention scores, and that there were no interactions of age and initial level (i.e. the benefits of being younger were not different for higher scorers). Table 4.2 shows the means and standard errors calcu-

TABLE 4.2

Mean Percentage Retention for a 30-year-old Subject on the Immediate Memory Task, Together with Range of Scores, Standard Errors, and Regression Coefficients for Age and Immediate Memory Score

	Mean	Range	Standard Errors	β (Age)	β (Immediate memory)
Story	78	0–105	20.50	−0.60	0.28
Faces	85.5	60–104	9.69	−0.43*	−1.05
Names	22.7	0–54	18.74	−0.49	3.50*
Words	52.2	0–70	11.86	−1.03**	1.11

*$P < .05$; ***$P < .001$ (one-tailed tests in all cases).

lated by regression equations, for 30-year-olds scoring at the mean on the immediate test, for the four tasks, which were retested after a week. The range of scores and regression coefficients for age and initial score are also given. The regression equations were used to establish deviations of individual retention scores from the expected score. Standard errors were corrected for deviation of the scores of the individual on the two predictor variables from the mean of the control group, as explained previously.

FIRST STUDY: 10 SUBJECTS CLAIMING SUPERIOR MEMORY ABILITY

As indicated at the beginning of this chapter, the first study carried out following the original investigation of TE's memory ability involved 10 subjects who volunteered following a radio appeal. This study was described by Wilding and Valentine (1988), using norms provided in the papers from which the tasks were derived, and data from some of the subjects were discussed further by Wilding and Valentine (1991), using norms from the first 17 subjects in the control group described in the previous section. This study failed to demonstrate exceptional memory ability over a range of tasks by any individual, though some subjects did show superior performance on isolated tasks, these differing for different subjects. In general, the islands of superiority appeared to match particular interests and prior practice, suggesting that unusual memory performance was due to acquired skills. However, none of these subjects reported any specific pre-learned memory strategies of the type employed by TE (and by several of the subjects tested later).

Table 4.3 gives raw scores and z scores, compared with age-matched norms from the control group, for the three subjects who produced between them most of the superior performances that occurred (the table differs slightly from Table 10.1 of Wilding and Valentine, 1991, because the norms are now based on 31 instead of 17 subjects in the control group). This table confirms the pattern previously demonstrated, showing the very uneven performance of subjects KC and (to a lesser extent) RR and the modest results of subject ED for immediate memory tasks.

One or more subjects from the control group equalled or outperformed these supposedly superior subjects on all but three of the tasks, when raw scores were compared. On immediate and delayed story recall KC's performance was best; he scored 116 and 99, while the best scores in the control group (obtained from two different subjects) were 114 and 95 for the immediate and delayed conditions respectively. On delayed recall of names to faces RR scored 8 and the best control subjects recalled only 4 names.

TABLE 4.3
Raw Scores and Deviations From the Control Group Mean (z), Adjusted for Age, for the
Three Subjects Performing Best Overall in the "Radio" Sample

	KC (35)		RR (42)		ED (67)	
	Raw	z	Raw	z	Raw	z
Story						
immediate	116	1.96	80	0.71	60	−0.22
delayed	99	1.73	70	0.88	84	1.94
Faces						
immediate	27	−2.69	35	0.10	36	1.09
delayed	19	−2.47	27	0.08	30	2.12
Names						
immediate	4	0.18	8	1.79	3	0.29
delayed	0	−0.90	8	5.42	3	2.19
Words						
immediate						
correct	15	−0.12	16	0.65	9	−0.08
intrusions	0	−1.34	0	−0.68	1	−0.49
delayed						
correct	5	−1.40	3	−1.59	5	1.60
intrusions	15	4.30	11	2.76	0	−1.70
Telephone numbers						
immediate	30	2.13	13	−0.01	6	−0.15
delayed	−	−	−		−	−
Prime Ministers						
correct	6	0.50	7.5	1.45	9	1.94
intrusions	2	3.77	0	−0.07	1	2.10
Pictures						
combined	11	0.22	11	0.40	7	−0.82
Snow crystals						
d'	0.67	−0.32	0.82	0.15	0.92	0.86
Beta	1.40	−0.33	1.21	−0.20	2.13	0.93
Mean z score						
immediate (7 tasks)[1]		0.19		0.54		0.14
delayed (4 tasks)[2]		−0.76		1.19		1.96

Mill Hill scores were not measured and have been set at the 50th percentile. Ages given in brackets after the initials of each subject. [1]Story, faces, names, words, telephone numbers, pictures, snow crystals; [2]story, faces, names, words.

TABLE 4.4
Percentage Retained Over a Week and *z* Scores for Difference between Obtained and
Predicted Score on the Delayed Tests

	KC		RR		ED	
	%	*z*	%	*z*	%	*z*
Story	85	0.22	87	0.70	140	3.71
Faces	70	−1.88	77	−0.41	83	1.45
Names	0	−1.12	100	6.31	100	3.55
Words	33	−1.00	19	−1.72	56	2.70
Mean	47	0.95	71	1.22	95	2.85

Predicted delayed scores were calculated by regression equations including age and initial score as predictor variables; *z* scores were calculated employing standard errors corrected for deviation from the mean of the control group on the predictor variables.

Inspection of the *z* scores, which are adjusted for age, highlights the unusual delayed memory performance of ED. This is further confirmed by calculating retention scores, that is the percentage of the original recall achieved after a week's delay (Table 4.4). ED's retention score was superior to every other subject on the story, was matched only by RR on the names and she was outperformed by only a single subject (from the control group) on the words. On the face recognition task, one subject in the superior group and one in the control group both achieved perfect retention (but only recognised 27 and 25 faces respectively in the immediate test, compared with 36 for ED) and several subjects had higher percentage retention than ED. The *z* scores in Table 4.4 indicate performance when age is taken into account (ED was aged 67) and demonstrate still more clearly the outstanding level of her retention.

Conclusions from the First Study

Superior performance was not restricted to the group claiming superior memory ability and was not apparent over a range of tasks in the case of any individual, so the study provided no support for any general memory ability. There was, however, one exception to this picture, namely the delayed recall of subject ED. When compared with age-corrected norms, she displayed consistently high performance on the four delayed memory tasks, with an average standard deviate score of 1.96, equivalent to 3.92 standard deviations above the expected mean (if all scores are assumed to be independent). The delayed memory tasks covered a range of material (story, faces, names, words), so ED's retention gives every appearance of being a general superiority in one of the components of memory discussed in Chapter 3. Her average percentage loss over the week was 5%, compared with 50% for the control group as a whole and 54% for the other five subjects in the "superior" group who completed all the delayed memory tasks. Compared with age-corrected norms for retention, calculated in the way explained earlier, her retention was 5.7 standard deviations above the expected mean.

This evidence is particularly striking in view of ED's unremarkable performance on the immediate memory tasks, where only the face recognition results showed even a modest departure from the normal age-corrected mean. ED did not report using any special strategies and, if she had been using these, the effects would surely have been more apparent for immediate testing than for delayed testing. She claimed she had a "very good memory" and in one important sense of the term her results confirmed this claim. Her performance was quantitatively superior to normals but not so superior as to be qualitatively different in the manner attainable by the use of special strategies for immediate recall, such as has been demonstrated in several of the cases discussed earlier.

TWO UNUSUAL INDIVIDUALS

In the period between the initial study just described, with its rather disappointing results for our aim of identifying individuals with markedly superior memory ability, and the larger study described in the next chapter, we tested two individuals who both displayed highly unusual memory ability but showed very different patterns in their performance. One showed superior (though not always remarkably superior) performance over the whole range of tasks in our battery, without employing any highly practised strategies, while the other brought to the tasks highly developed techniques, which had been employed in learning 15,000 telephone numbers. This second subject's results also raised intriguing questions about the possibility of some pre-existing natural ability underpinning the technique.

The contrast between these two subjects first highlighted many of the questions aired earlier and provided the background for our main study of competitors at the First World Memory Championships.

Two additional tasks were introduced with the first of these subjects and two more with the second. These were:

The Individual Differences Questionnaire (Paivio & Harshman, 1983), which measures self-reported tendencies to verbal and imaginal thinking (henceforth referred to as the IDQ).

TABLE 4.5
Raw Scores on Each Memory Task and Deviations (z), Compared with a Control Group
Subject Aged 30, for JR, TM, and TE

	JR (17)		*TM (24)*		*TE (25)*	
	Raw	z	Raw	z	Raw	z
Story						
immediate	105	1.47	18	−1.72	131	2.42
delayed	90	1.23	5	−1.71	127	2.55
Faces						
immediate	36	0.06	34	−0.56	36	0.06
delayed	35	1.62	30	0.27	−	−
Names						
immediate	12	3.07	10.5	2.51	7	1.22
delayed	12	7.57	0	−1.00	12	7.57
Words						
immediate						
correct	22	1.79	24	2.42		
intrusions	0	−1.33	0	−1.33		
delayed						
correct	21	4.60	19	3.80		
intrusions	0	−1.46	1	−1.07		
Telephone numbers						
immediate	19	0.41	36	2.74		
delayed	−					
Prime Ministers						
correct	3	−1.47	4	−0.78		
intrusions	0	−0.06	0	−0.06		
Pictures						
combined	14	1.43	11.5	0.35		
Snow crystals						
d′	1.52	1.35	1.75	1.83		
Beta	2.42	0.11	3.40	0.64		
Mean z score						
immediate (7 tasks)		1.37		1.08		
delayed (4 tasks)		3.76		0.34		
Age of earliest memory	7.0	1.51	4.0	0.26		
Mill Hill percentile	−	−	50	0		
IDQ						
verbal	21	−0.27	32	2.79	21	0.28
imaginal	32	4.81	35	5.87	32	4.81
VVIQ (eyes open)	−		75	1.05		

A Number Matrix   (eight rows of six items each), previously used with VP and TE (Gordon et al., 1984) shown for as long as the subject wished; recall was then attempted. If this was incorrect further learning time was given. Time to read and recall the whole matrix correctly was measured, in order to determine whether recall appeared to be based on a visual image; forward and backward recall of certain rows and columns was requested and timed as a further test of this possibility.

The Vividness of Visual Imagery Questionnaire   (Marks, 1973), which requires self-report of the vividness of specified images, first with eyes open, then with eyes closed, from which a total vividness score is derived (henceforth referred to as the VVIQ).

The Mill Hill Vocabulary Scale, Part B,   which requires synonyms to be selected for target words from six possibilities. A total score and age-adjusted percentile score are derived.

JR

Results for this 17-year old subject were described briefly by Wilding and Valentine (1991). Table 4.5 presents her raw scores and z scores compared with norms for 30-year-olds derived from the control group (see p. 95 for the reason for using norms from 30-year olds).

JR is, in many ways, the most interesting subject we have tested. Her mean performance over seven immediate memory tasks was 3.87 standard deviations above the expected mean. This performance will be compared with those of subjects from the World Memory Championships later, but some indication of her ability is shown by the fact that on the three tasks that had been given to TE she did as well as him on immediate face recognition (performing at ceiling), but better than him on immediate recall of names to faces (12 compared with 7 correct), and equally well on delayed recall of these (12 names out of 13 correct). Only on recall of the story was she clearly inferior to TE. Furthermore, unlike TE, she

---

Notes on Table 4.5

Mean and standard deviation from original studies: IDQ verbal: mean 22.0, *SD* 3.59, maximum 47; IDQ imaginal: mean 18.4, *SD* 2.83, maximum 39.

VVIQ (normally scored from 16 to 80, with low scores indicating high imagery, but scores have been reversed here so that high scores reflect high imagery): mean 62.7, *SD* 11.76, range 16–80.

No Mill Hill score was taken for JR, and TM scored at the 50th percentile on the Mill Hill, so norms have been adjusted to the 50th percentile. Scores are also given for the psychometric tests and deviation (z) compared with the means given in the original sources.

TABLE 4.6
Percentage Retained Over a Week and Deviation from the
Control Group (z) for JR and TM

	JR		TM	
	%	z	%	z
Story	86	0.13	28	−0.39
Faces	97	1.36	88	0.12
Names	100	7.73	0	−3.44
Words	95	4.85	79	3.35
Mean	95	3.52	49	−0.09

reported no special strategies for face recognition or name learning. She did link the words in the free recall task into a story but this was the only case in which she reported any form of mnemonic method. It appears to have been devised on the spot for this specific task rather than prepared beforehand for use in several different situations.

Impressive though JR's immediate memory performance was, the most striking aspect of her ability was her very high retention on the delayed recall tasks (Table 4.6). Her average percentage loss on the four tasks, like ED's, was 5% (7.04 standard deviations above the expected retention level for 30-year-olds) and this finding offers further support for the earlier suggestion that superior retention is a specific component of superior natural memory performance in some individuals. One other subject showing a similar low level of forgetting will be described later. It should be emphasised again that the delayed recall tasks were given without warning and, while there is no irrefutable proof that subjects showing superior retention had not rehearsed in the interval, none of these subjects indicated that they had expected a delayed test and rehearsed accordingly.

JR also attempted to learn the matrix of 6 × 8 digits, but after 514 seconds of study she could only recall 37/48 digits correctly. Since the task was not carried out by control subjects it is not possible to compare this with any norms. Data are given later from several subjects who did learn the matrix very rapidly and of course VP and TE both achieved this.

The main object of the matrix learning task was to test whether subjects could encode the matrix as a visual image. Time to recall was compared with time to read out the figures from a visual display, and time to recall rows and columns in the normal direction was compared with time to recall them in a backwards direction. The rationale for these comparisons was that, if a visual image were employed, recall should be as fast as reading, and forward and backward recall should each take about the same time. As JR did not memorise the matrix successfully, only very limited tests of this type were possible. She recalled somewhat more *quickly* in reverse order (8 seconds for backward recall of row 8 compared with 10, 14, and 19 seconds for forward recall of rows 1, 2, and 5, and 8 seconds for recall of column 1 in the upward direction compared with 10 seconds for downward recall). However, these times are sufficiently long to preclude the possibility that JR was recalling directly from any form of visual image, which would normally take about ½ second per item. Initially she denied that she was making use of any form of visual image, but when asked how she could recall at least as quickly in a backward as in a forward direction, she could offer no explanation but thought she might experience a type of visual image.

As will emerge in later discussion of the results obtained from some of the World Memory Championship subjects, with the possible exception of one of the subjects taking part in those championships, rapid and efficient learning of the matrix has only been observed when some special method of encoding digits has been mastered. No subject has emerged who has demonstrated any form of eidetic imagery, though a different form of image can, it seems, be created to aid recall once the matrix becomes well established in memory. JR's uncertainty about whether or not she experienced an image of the matrix may reflect an incomplete representation of this type, which depended on the incomplete propositional representation she had established of the matrix.

JR reported that one of her grandparents had a good memory for personal experiences. She was aware of her memory ability quite early in life, but her earliest reported memory occurred at the age of seven, long past the norm, which is around three years of age. She scored highly on both the imagery and verbal components of the IDQ. She was not given the VVIQ or Mill Hill vocabulary test.

TM

We first met TM in 1990 and reported our study of his memory in Wilding and Valentine (1994b) and have met him at intervals since. TM had achieved some fame as a memory expert by his ability to give the telephone number of any one of 15,000 Blackpool hotels in response to the hotel name. This was the main plank of an entertainment he gave around Blackpool during the summer season. The other elements were also mainly memory based and several depended on the same methods as he had employed to learn the hotel telephone numbers. He normally spent two to three hours a day in practising his method and rehearsing. Subsequent to our testing he has also offered a "Directory Enquiries" service for the whole of Blackpool.

On his own admission TM did not do well at school, nor were his relations with the rest of his family entirely satisfactory; they regarded him as eccentric and unwilling to settle down to proper work. He is convinced that his unusual abilities should equip him for some specialised job, but has found no niche that suits him or demands the exercise of his memory ability, other than offering entertainment. He would like to attain a world record for learning telephone numbers and show that his memory is worth something. He has, however, drifted between a variety of temporary and informal jobs and methods of earning his living—his cabaret-type show, taxi driving, advising a school for gifted children, appearances on television, and he has also contemplated taking a psychology degree. The most obvious role for a memory expert in our society is as a television performer or pundit (cf. Leslie Welch), but TM possesses no body of knowledge that suits him for this role and has no great ability to settle on such a goal (other than the learning of telephone numbers!) and persist in working towards it.

For him, he says, numbers are like words and are more important to him than people. They evoke meanings and sensory associations and he likes to go through them to stimulate each sense, savouring the colours and tastes they elicit. He admits that he has difficulties in social interchange. He does not read books, but gave two somewhat conflicting reasons for this. One was that he got bored and the other was that they evoked too many associations and confused him. The parallels between TM's reported experiences and Luria's account of S are frequently striking.

He relates that he first developed his memory method at the age of 21 after an experience when walking home one evening. A passing car splashed mud over him, which greatly annoyed him. While grumbling to himself he realised that he could recall the number of the car and during the rest of his walk home he practised memorising the numbers of other passing cars and found he could do this easily. He claims he used simple mnemonic methods but it is unclear what these were or where he got the ideas from, so the question of whether he does possess some unusual natural memory ability is difficult to answer. He himself believed for a time that his achievements were all due to strategy but this view is at variance with his untutored ability to memorise the car numbers and in a recent communication he seems to admit that there may be more to his memory than sheer graft.

For his public performance TM carries out the following tasks:

- He asks the first name of each member of the audience; later in the show he selects individuals at random and recalls their name.
- He asks individuals the date of their birth and then tells them the day of the week on which they were born.
- He distributes pages of the Blackpool telephone directory (*Yellow Pages*) and asks members of the audience to call out names of hotels, then gives the telephone number.
- Using his left hand, he writes in mirror writing names or words called out by the audience.
- He carries out multiplication of numbers called out by the audience or calculates squares or square roots.
- He distributes a pack of playing cards face up among the audience, then selects individuals at random and tells them what card they are holding.

TM explained how he carried out each of these tasks.

Names As each person announces their name, he retrieves an image of a person he knows with the same name and links the two. He claims that long practice has enabled him to do this quickly and reliably.

Dates of Birth. After long experience TM knows instantly that certain dates fell on certain days and this enables him to give an immediate answer in many cases. In other cases he uses a method on which he originally depended for all his answers. Every year and month has been assigned a code number between 0 and 6 and he has learned these for the whole period from 1900 to 2000, making use of his method of learning numbers, which is described later. Codes for date, month, and year are added together and divided by 7; the remainder gives the day of the week. For example 27 October 1964 yields $27 + 1 + 3 = 31$. After division by 7 the remainder is 3 and the third day of the week is Tuesday.

Telephone Numbers. TM's method of learning numbers is the key to most of his performance. He has learned a readily imageable associate to every number between 00 and 99: 00 is a bicycle, 39 is Hitler, 57 is tomato sauce. Larger numbers are broken down into digit pairs and the images for each pair are combined into a memorable image such as Hitler holding a bottle of tomato sauce (3957). TM says he can retain the order of the digits because each compound image has a temporal pattern; for example Hitler holds out his hand and receives the bottle of tomato sauce. When learning telephone numbers of hotels, the hotel name is represented by another image which is combined with the image repre-

Fig. 4.4.   Mnemonic for the number 395700.

senting the telephone number. Thus "The Beeches" might be represented by a group of trees from which Hitler emerges holding a bottle of tomato sauce and jumps on a bicycle (395700) as illustrated in Fig. 4.4.

TM has a remarkable facility in generating associations and images. We showed him a list of pharmacological terms from a first-year medical lecture and he rapidly recoded these unknown words into a kaleidoscope of short familiar words with similar sounds, uttering them too quickly for the results to be audible on our recording system! To what extent this is learned and how far he already possessed expertise in generating and controlling imagery before beginning to study mnemonics is a tantalising but probably unanswerable question.

Mirror Writing.   He has developed this skill in much the same way as any other motor skill is acquired, but is still considerably less fluent than in normal writing.

Multiplication.   Mental arithmetic was achieved by breaking the problem into small manageable components and retaining the original numbers and intermediate totals in images of the same type as those used for telephone numbers. Hence, to calculate 3957 squared, the number is first stored as Hitler with his now familiar bottle of tomato sauce, then broken down into 3000^2, 3000×900, 3000×50, 3000×7, 900×3000, etc. As each step is carried out the subtotal is stored as a further image. Thus 3000^2 yields 9,000,000, broken down by TM into 09 00 00 00 and stored as the symbol for 09 (a liner, because "nine is a line") plus three bicycles. 3000×900 added to this running total yields 11 70 00 00 (two pints of beer, something travelling fast, like a vehicle doing the maximum speed on the motorway, and two bicycles). 3000×50 is then calculated, the result is added in, and the new running total coded, and so on. Hence, the performance depends heavily on the ability to encode numbers into a form in which they are easily retained while performing other arithmetical operations.

Memory for Cards.   Each card has a code consisting of a number for the suit, which is sequentially combined with the number on the card. Hearts is 1, so the 3 of Hearts is 13, the 9 of Hearts is 19 (and the 10 of Hearts is 20). These numbers are transformed into the codes already described (13 is a ladder, by the association with bad luck). The cards are distributed in an already memorised order, so TM simply has to remember the starting point of the distribution (or perhaps two or three starting points if they were not distributed in a continuous sequence) in order to work out what card any member of the audience is holding. Again it is the memory system that is at the heart of the demonstration.

TM drove most of the night in order to meet us, only getting about two hours sleep. We were concerned that this might affect his memory, but he assured us that it normally had little effect. Having explained his methods as outlined previously, he demonstrated their efficacy by giving days of birth correctly in response to both our birth dates, gave correct telephone numbers for three randomly chosen hotels in Blackpool, and rapidly carried out several complex calculations. From the explanations he provided, it was clear that he depended primarily on prelearned codes for converting numbers into concrete objects, or years and months into numbers with special properties, or playing cards into numbers. Combined with these basic tools, he possessed, or had developed, the ability to generate associates and images very rapidly which was referred to above. We were therefore interested to discover how he would handle those of our memory tasks that were not immediately amenable to these methods.

TM's results are shown in Tables 4.5 and 4.6, with those of JR. His results on the number matrix are presented in the next chapter, for comparison with the subjects to be described there. He did well on immediate recall of names to faces, immediate and delayed recall of words and telephone numbers, and on the number matrix and snow crystals. On the other tasks his performance was moderate (faces, pictures) or appalling (story, delayed recall of names). In general, he did well on tasks that were amenable to his methods. However, he commented that he normally learns first names to faces, so learning surnames required an extension of his method, and the fast presentation rate gave him little time for discriminating the faces. He learned the words in order, using "One is a bun", etc. to anchor the positions and associating images from the rhyme with images derived from the words. Again, he found the speed of presentation was too fast to enable thorough use of this strategy. Telephone numbers were learned in his standard manner. With the snow crystals he tried to find a distinctive feature and associate, but soon found that several of the stimuli were rather similar and that more than one feature really needed to be employed in order to discriminate the stimuli efficiently.

On the tasks that elicited less impressive performance, he remarked that photographs of faces provided minimal information and did not encourage vivid associations, especially at the rate of presentation used. To retain the spatial and temporal positions of the pictures, he tried to use the "One is a bun" rhyme to retain the temporal positions, then associate the picture being shown with an image from the rhyme. Spatial positions were encoded as houses in a terrace. He performed much better on the latter (achieving a perfect mean score of 8) than on the former (mean score 3.5), suggesting he was focusing attention on the spatial information.

TM's delayed recall was uneven, being impressive only on the word list. His retention, likewise, when compared with norms adjusted for age and initial score, ranged from excellent on the word list to very poor on the names.

The poor performance on the story, compared with the other tasks, could have been due to it being the first task given. TM was somewhat anxious about what he would be required to do. However, his main problem seemed to lie in a failure to understand the sequence of events and an overconcentration on applying mnemonic methods. When he was first asked to recall the story he stated that he had no comprehension of what had happened in it. This was reminiscent of S's problems, reported by Luria, and TM's own comment that he did not read books because they evoked too many associations. To determine whether this weakness was an isolated case, he was tested on the same story two years later, without giving him any indication that he had heard it before. He scored 56, a considerable improvement but still a modest score (0.34 standard deviations below the norm for a 30-year-old, falling at the 37th percentile). He was also given "Circle Island" (Thorndyke, 1977) after a further year and did better, scoring 17 (0.36 standard deviations above the mean for a group of 17-year-olds).

In order to discover whether TM had a problem in processing (and hence recalling) meaning, compared with his exceptional performance when required to reproduce words or numbers literally, his comprehension of non-literal aspects of language was tested with tasks from the Right Hemisphere Language Battery (Bryant, 1989) designed to test right hemisphere damage in stroke patients. Four tests were selected, examining ability to understand metaphorical meaning (two tests), ability to infer meaning from prose, and appreciation of humour.

The first test of comprehension of metaphor required TM to choose a picture to match a metaphorical sentence such as "She weighed her words carefully." A set of four pictures was presented, illustrating the metaphorical meaning and the literal meaning plus two other unrelated pictures. The second test of metaphor comprehension required selection of a sentence to explain a metaphor, with three possible sentences being offered, one giving the metaphorical meaning, one the literal, and the other being a filler sentence. Ability to make inferences was tested by questions, which could only be answered by making deductions from a short prose passage that did not include the answers directly. The humour test required selection of a punch line from four possibilities to complete a joke.

TM showed no evidence of a problem in understanding non-literal aspects of language. He scored 10/10, 10/10, 10/12, and 9/10 compared with norms in the manual of 9.53 (SD 0.63), 9.67 (0.71), 9.16 (0.56), and 9.70 (0.47). The tasks are easy for normal subjects, having been designed for use with stroke patients, so there is a possibility that they were insufficiently sensitive to detect some weakness in TM's ability, but if his problem required more sensitive tests to detect it, it would be unlikely to explain his very weak performance on the story recall. Hence, it seems more likely that the latter was due to inappropriate reliance on his methods in a task that was highly unsuited to them.

However, we are reluctant to accept that this offers a sufficient explanation, since at the very least it gives no insight into why TM should process meaningful material so differently from most people. The resemblance of his account of his mental life to that of S has already been noted and also shows some parallels to the physically bound memories of some autistics. In other respects TM's general behaviour, his inability to relax or stop talking, his sudden switching of attention to peripheral and irrelevant stimuli, and his problems in pursuing a meaningful conversation were reminiscent of both Attention Deficit Disorder and Tourette's Syndrome.

TM originally believed that his memory ability depended completely on his pre-learned methods. At one point he was writing a guide to these methods which he believed would allow anyone to develop a memory like his, but he came to have doubts about the general efficacy of such training. He wrote (personal communication):

After spending 3 months compiling notes on how to develop memory using my mnemonics, I noticed and realised a major flaw and that is the fact that my method is useless to the man in the street, but is only suitable for use and understanding for those who possess a remarkable imagination in which they not only can physically visualise but can also incorporate into the image smells, tastes, sounds, textures and many other concepts.

TM certainly possesses a "remarkable imagination", as shown by his ability to produce associations and images to the most unpromising material. His account of his earliest memory was unusually detailed and visually explicit. It went as follows:

My earliest memory is of childhood and sitting in a chair and looking up and down the garden of our house ... The year is probably about 1966, June. Now I remember looking up the garden. We've got a small swimming pool. We've got the big slide. We've got a big cable car. All of these objects are of fantastic proportions, everything is greatly exaggerated, of fantastic size. And I'm looking up the garden. The garden seems as if it's, what, about 100 yards, when in fact it's only 30 or 40.

The image is very blurred. I see colours, I see a big fence. Now I know that this fence was not built until 1969, so it's probably a figment of my imagination added in. I see a chicken ranch which wasn't built till 1969. But I see this and everything which appears, everything in my childhood, all the things I'm familiar with are laid out in front of me.

While it is impossible to establish whether this scene has been refreshed experientially or verbally since the original experience, the account certainly suggests an unusually vivid representation. He scored extremely highly on both imaginal and verbal thinking and well towards the vivid end of the VVIQ scale. On the other hand TM's performance was not such as to suggest a natural ability which produced excellent memory performance over a wide range of tasks. His performance was very variable, being most obviously superior where his methods could be most readily deployed (names, words, telephone numbers, number matrix), was good on some other tasks (spatial position of pictures, recognition of snow crystals), was unimpressive on face recognition, though vivid imagery should have been beneficial, and finally was very poor on the story and temporal sequence of pictures. It may well be significant that the Circle Island story, on which he performed much better (though not with distinction), is a logically ordered and relatively straightforward series of events, without any supernatural elements, metamorphosis of a main character, or scope for reordering of the temporal sequence. Our conclusion was that TM is over-reliant on his mnemonic methods, so that his performance will vary with the suitability of the task to the narrow range of methods he employs. The more structured the material to be memorised and the greater the scope for literal memorisation, the better TM will perform.

A further question about TM, which arises in many such cases, is what motivated him to undertake the immense labours of developing and applying his methods. Undoubtedly part of the driving force was his belief that he did possess unusual abilities, combined with his inability to perform well at school, leading to a determination to demonstrate that he could succeed at the highest level in something. The rather sad corollary is that the field of his success offers very limited opportunity for wider achievement, a disappointment also experienced by Luria's subject S.

TM's performance on the number matrix is discussed later, where it is compared with that of other subjects. His scores on the Mill Hill vocabulary test, IDQ, and VVIQ are shown in Table 4.4. His Mill Hill score was exactly average, but he scored at a very high level on both components of Paivio and Harshman's IDQ questionnaire and reported very vivid imagery on the VVIQ. As usual, it is impossible to decide categorically whether this reflects practice in his method (which depends heavily on facility in imagery) or some natural facility. The description of his earliest memory and of experiencing colours and tastes in response to numbers suggest some pre-existing unusual aspects to his sensory experience, which may have been accentuated subsequently through practice.

OVERVIEW

JR and TM illustrate the difficulty of drawing any general conclusions about superior memory performance. JR's ability was apparently almost entirely independent of methods and practice, and was demonstrated across almost all the tasks attempted. Her lowest z score of only 0.06 on immediate recognition of faces in fact represented a maximum score on a task on which even control group performance was at a high level; the task was too easy and superior performance could not therefore be demonstrated. Her retention on four tasks over a week was enormously superior to that of the control group (and most other subjects we have tested). She was aware from a young age that her memory was good and at least one member of her family possessed similar ability. We did not at this stage of the research administer the Mill Hill vocabulary test or VVIQ, so had no objective measures of her general cognitive ability or imagery ability.

TM's most striking performances were due to his method, apart possibly from the snow crystals test, where he used only a very general method of searching for distinctive features. On some other tests he did badly and his retention over a week was unimpressive (51% average loss). The experience that awakened his interest in memory occurred at the age of 21 and he cited no relative with any similar ability. Nevertheless, he did possess, whether naturally or through practice is unclear, unusual abilities to generate images and associations, as shown by informal demonstrations and supported by his account of his earliest memory and his VVIQ score. His Mill Hill vocabulary score was, however, only average.

On the basis of the evidence available, it seems necessary to conclude that both strategically based and naturally based superiority in memory may occur. A great deal of the evidence available is ambiguous, as has been discussed at length already. It is impossible to prove conclusively the absence of any strategy or method, hence the doubts about the underlying causes of Shereshevskii's and VP's superiority. The most convincing cases of naturally based superiority, apart from Aitken, have been based on results with specific tasks or materials (Coltheart & Glick, 1974; Gummerman & Gray, 1971; Thompson et al., 1991). However, our initial studies have provided some suggestive leads, especially the high retention ability of ED, also demonstrated by JR in combination with excellent performance at the immediate memory tasks. It may be true that ED's claim of a "very good memory" might have been verified if her performance on immediate memory tasks had been tested at a younger age.

At this point in our research it seemed very difficult to advance the investigations further by trying to gather data from other cases of superior memory with a view to establishing whether the emerging picture could be clarified and confirmed. The chance to carry the work further came some years later when we were fortunate to gain access to competitors at the First World Memory Championships in London in October 1992. Seven individuals had entered for these championships, all of whom agreed to carry out our tasks. Through them we also made contact with others who had been in the audience and claimed to have good memories. As a result we were able to carry out a study using the tasks we have described, together with a few additions, in order to gather a more substantial body of data on memory ability in a sizeable group of experts, who had achieved high standards in public competition or were believed to be able to perform at a similar level. The next chapter will describe this larger study.

5 Memory Champions

The First World Memory Championships (or Memoriad) were held in London in October 1991. The main organiser, Tony Buzan, hoped to publicise methods of improving memory and allied abilities and to generate interest in publications and organisations concerned with developing such techniques. The Second Memoriad was held in August 1993 and the third such event took place in August 1994. All three events have been held in London and, to date, all competitors have come from the British Isles. Competitors entered in response to public advertisements, and usually participated in all events. Performance was ranked on each event and the ranks were summed across events to decide the overall winner. Considerable publicity has been generated in the British media, and the winner of the 1991 and 1993 events, Dominic O'Brien, has won considerable sums by employing his memory methods playing blackjack at gambling casinos, from many of which he is now banned as a result. He has also built a "media" career on his success, including writing a book about his method (O'Brien, 1993). The 1994 winner was Jonathan Hancock, who has written two books (1995, 1996). It has to be admitted, however, that watching the furrowed brows of people memorising is unlikely to achieve the status of a major spectator sport, even though spectators are invited to attempt the tasks themselves. Interest in the event has yet to spread further abroad.

At the first Memoriad, seven competitors entered and undertook tasks of recalling the names of the audience (about 50 people), lists of numbers and words, chess positions, a piece of text, nonsense syllables, and a pack of cards. In some sequential recall tasks, recall was only scored up to the first error, irrespective of performance after this point.

Dominic O'Brien based his performance entirely on the method of loci, having prepared more than 30 different routes, with different numbers of locations in each, appropriate for tasks of different length. O'Brien had seen another of the competitors, Creighton Carvello, on television some four years previously, demonstrating his ability to memorise perfectly the order of a pack of cards as quickly as possible, and decided to emulate him. Carvello held the world record for the speed of performing this task for many years, until O'Brien displaced him.

With the co-operation of Tony Buzan, we were able to contact all the competitors after the event and ask if they would be willing to undertake our own battery of tasks, described in the previous chapter. These were much more varied than those used at the Memoriad. All agreed and we were also able to contact a further three subjects who had been spectators at the event (being interested in memory performance) and had been able to perform well on the tasks given to the competitors.

As well as undertaking our battery of memory tasks, these subjects also answered questions about their ability and methods (Table 5.1) and completed the Mill Hill Vocabulary Scale Part B (Synonyms), the VVIQ, and the IDQ questionnaires. Surprisingly, not all the competitors claimed

TABLE 5.1
Answers to the Background Questions from the 10 Subjects

| | Subject | | | | | | | | | |
	A	B	C	D	E	F	G	H	I	J
Sex	M	M	M	F	M	M	M	M	M	M
Age	53	27	34	28	33	35	19	47	30	13
Good natural memory	y	y	?	y	?	y	y	y	n	y
Early awareness	y	y	?	y	y	y	y	y	n	y
Techniques	n	n	y	n	n	y	y	y	y	n
Regular practice	n	n	y	n	n	n	y	y	y	n
Use in job, etc.	n	n	y	n	n	y?	y	y	y	n
Vivid imagery	y	y	?	y	y	n	y	y	n	y
Near relative	y	y	y	y	n	n	y	n	n	y

y = Yes, n = No.

to be using prepared strategies, either during the competition or on our tasks. Some relied on what they believed to be a naturally superior memory ability. The problem of evaluating self-reports about memory techniques is a thorny one, which will be discussed in more detail later.

THE SUBJECTS

A brief description of each subject and the answers they provided to the preliminary questions will now be given. Unless otherwise stated, all subjects took part in the Memoriad. Note that, inevitably, these statements could not be checked in many cases, but they provide some insight into the background and views of the subjects. It should be borne in mind that many of the points are self-reported views, but we will avoid constantly stressing this.

Subject A, aged 53, had been the subject of a number of recent press items concerning his ability to recall nearly all the telephone exchange codes of the British Isles in response to town names. He had memorised these during his job as a telephone operator. In fact, a few informal tests showed that his performance on these was by no means perfect. He had grown up in Nigeria, but his memory ability was not the result of having been reared in a culture with a strong oral tradition. He had a good memory as a boy and had been encouraged to learn a wide variety of facts. He did not practise any special memory techniques, but said that he could see the telephone numbers or recall their sound, usually in groups of three. He said he could see them on a white screen and read them backwards, but in fact he performed backward recall more slowly than would be suggested by this claim. He claimed that he was also good at remembering routes and short spoken phrases in a foreign language (which he could repeat with an almost perfect accent). He believed that memory depended mainly on interest in the material being memorised.

Subject B, aged 27, was a mathematician working in a financial institution, with a particularly good memory for numbers, but he also stated that he had a good natural memory for visual, tactile, and musical material. He made no systematic use of mnemonic methods, though he occasionally employed ad hoc methods to aid memory; he believed his ability was mainly natural, particularly as his father "forgot nothing till he was 50" and one of his uncles also displayed similar ability.

Subject C, aged 34, an airport cleaning supervisor, had only developed his interest in memory improvement a few years previously and had devoted a great deal of effort to practising the method of loci since then. He did not believe that he had any exceptional natural memory ability. However, his brother, a Sanskrit scholar, had demonstrated ability to acquire new vocabulary very rapidly, having once learned 1000 words in a week.

Subject D, a 28-year old journalist, did not take part in the Memoriad, nor did she practise any memory methods. She was the only female subject in the study; her sister did some of the tasks but did not complete the study. She had found memorising school work easy, for example learning languages, and was good at mastering accent, but had also found she could rote learn science fairly easily in order to pass exams, though she had no interest in or understanding of it. She thought her sense of direction and memory for spatial relations was poor. Several of her relatives had extremely good memories.

Subject E, aged 33, worked as a business consultant. He made no systematic use of practised memory methods, stating that he used "brute" memory most of the time. He did, however, invent methods of memorising complex numbers on the spot, as he did for the matrix we presented. At school he had found his memory was good and he claimed that he experienced vivid images. His work required problem solving and creative abilities; he believed that other members of his family were also endowed with such abilities, rather than with superior memory.

Subject F, aged 35, did not take part in the Memoriad, but was interested in mnemonic methods for his work as a magician and hypnotist. He used the figure alphabet and key words for memorising playing cards; he started learning these when he was 13 years' old, though he did not spend large amounts of time practising these methods. He thought his memory for routes was good, though he did not claim any strong imagery. He said he was bad at remembering to do things.

Subject G, a 19-year old student of English, claimed that his natural memory, in common with other members of his family, was very good and he had "always" known this. His imagery was very vivid, but he had also developed several mnemonic methods since the age of 16, based principally on a method of recoding numbers into sentences, combined with the method of loci. He had also learned to associate each playing card of the pack with a specific word. He practises mainly before entering competitions, but also occasionally at other times, in order to maintain facility in his methods and improve control of his imagery. "One thing I do," he stated, "is to pick a reasonably long word and hold it in my mind clearly enough to read it forwards and backwards, pick out, say, all the alternate letters and even rearrange the letters, making anagrams etc."

Subject H, aged 47, is a nurse. He has long experience of methods for improving memory, which he has been practising regularly since he was seven years' old. He frequently competes in memory contests and attempts world records, especially in the speed of memorising a pack of cards. He said that he had a good memory at school for facts, stories, and conversations.

Subject I, aged 30, claimed that his natural memory was "terrible". He teaches methods of memory improvement, in which he has been interested since he was 18, when he read a book entitled *Practical Way to a Better Memory* by Bruno Furst. He uses the methods frequently in his work but does not practise them intensively.

Subject J, aged 13, attended the Memoriad as a spectator and found that he could perform as well as the competitors in many of the tasks. He entered the second Memoriad as a competitor. His only strategic methods were commonsense ones developed on the spot, such as rehearsing numbers in groups.

All these subjects but one were male and most of them were in the 20–35 age range. The earlier study of JR, and the data from Subject D in the present study, demonstrate that good memory performance is not a prerogative of males. It is likely that the competitive nature of the occasion was responsible for the predominant features and rather uniform nature of the sample.

RESULTS

Memory Tasks

Table 5.2 presents the raw scores for the 10 subjects, who will be referred to as the expert sample from now on. In Table 5.3 these have been converted to z scores compared with the performance of the control group and adjusted for age and Mill Hill score. A mean z score is also given for the seven immediate and four delayed tasks as an indication of overall performance. The expected mean z score for the seven immediate tasks (if performance on these were independent) is of course 0 with a standard deviation of $1/7$ (i.e. 0.38) and the corresponding figure for the four delayed tasks is again 0 with a standard deviation of $1/4$ (i.e. 0.5). The tables indicate that Subjects G, I, C, D, and H all achieved a mean z score on the seven immediate tasks of 1.05 or greater, some 2½ standard deviations above the expected mean. On the delayed tasks there were fewer examples of outstanding performance, the highest means being achieved by Subjects D and J (both at least 2 standard deviations above the expected mean) and B and G (1.6 standard deviations above the expected mean).

Performance in relation to the control group was also evaluated by ranking all subjects (ignoring age differences) on each task, then calculating the mean of these ranks and ranking these means to indicate level of overall performance (i.e. the lowest mean was given an overall

TABLE 5.2
Scores of the Subjects on Each Task

					Subject					
	A	*B*	*C*	*D*	*E*	*F*	*G*	*H*	*I*	*J*
Story										
immediate	113	102	91	132	75	105	104	29	122	77
delayed	89	98	44	100	70	69	91	26	–	71
Faces										
immediate	31	32	36	33	35	35	36	36	34	33
delayed	17	30	27	33	28	22	28	25	–	33
Names										
immediate	1	7	13	13	0	4	13	7	12	6
delayed	0	2	2	5	0	3	3	3	–	4
Words										
immediate										
correct	8	19.5	25	16	21	19.5	25	23	22	16
intrusions	0	0	0	0	1	1	0	0	0	0
delayed										
correct	3	12	15	12	9	4.5	12	2	–	12
intrusions	0	7	7	1	6	1	1	16	–	7
Telephone numbers										
immediate	12	36	36	27	24	8	35	36	36	19
delayed	–	24	8	–	0	0	–	16	–	2
Prime Ministers										
correct	9	–	7	5	9	9	9	6	6	3
intrusions	0	–	0	0	0	0	0	2	0	0
Pictures										
spatial	5.5	4.0	5.0	7.0	7.0	8.0	7.0	6.5	8.0	5.5
temporal	2.0	3.5	3.0	6.0	5.5	8.0	4.5	3.0	4.0	2.5
Snow crystals										
d'	0.90	1.44	1.17	1.31	1.28	0.96	1.95	1.17	1.28	0.77
Beta	1.77	1.77	1.90	1.87	2.27	1.88	3.26	1.90	2.27	1.77

rank of 1, the next lowest an overall rank of 2 and so forth). For this assessment JR and TM, described in the previous chapter, were also included, giving a total of 43 subjects in all. Table 5.4 presents the mean ranks and overall ranking for all 12 expert subjects (10 from the present study plus JR and TM). On the immediate memory tasks, 7 of the first 11 places were occupied by subjects from this group (G, JR, I, D, C, TM, H), but subjects from the control group occupied positions 5, 8, and equal 10th. Subjects A, B, E, and F did not achieve high ranks.

TABLE 5.3

z Scores for Each Subject for Each Memory Task, Adjusted for Age and Mill Hill Score, Plus Mean z Scores for Seven Immediate Memory Tasks and for Four Delayed Memory Tasks

	Subject									
	A	B	C	D	E	F	G	H	I	J [2]
Story										
immediate	1.80	0.54	0.69	1.62	0.12	0.75	0.63	−1.16	1.44	
delayed	1.64	0.95	−0.55	0.98	0.42	0.04	0.71	−0.60	−	
Faces										
immediate	−0.61	−0.49	0.50	−0.12	0.09	0.64	0.80	0.56	0.06	
delayed	−2.47	−0.13	−0.62	0.67	−0.37	−2.14	−0.69	−0.37	−	
Names										
immediate	−0.87	0.90	3.52	3.16	−1.51	−0.17	3.19	1.51	2.87	
delayed	−0.37	0.47	0.61	2.77	−1.07	1.43	1.24	1.76	−	
Words										
immediate	−1.34	0.95	3.14	−0.20	1.74	1.30	2.75	3.30	1.80	
delayed	−0.25	1.66	3.01	1.69	0.31	−1.05	1.64	−1.48	−	
Telephone numbers										
immediate	0.10	2.92	2.76	1.19	1.16	−1.35	2.37	3.47	2.58	
delayed[1]										
Prime Ministers	1.72	−	0.63	−1.61	2.20	1.33	1.41	0.17	−0.63	
Pictures										
combined	−0.87	−1.24	−1.06	1.25	0.95	2.77	0.56	−0.16	0.77	
Snow crystals										
d′	0.23	0.64	0.48	0.32	0.74	−0.31	1.76	0.95	0.37	
Mean										
immediate	−0.29	0.54	1.35	1.05	0.43	0.53	1.74	1.05	1.39	
delayed	−0.32	0.84	0.62	1.65	0.13	−0.38	0.82	−0.02	−	

[1] No z scores could be computed for delayed memory for telephone numbers as the control group found the task impossible, and did not attempt it.

[2] z scores were not computed for Subject J as his age was so far below the minimum of the control group.

On the four delayed tasks, Subjects JR, D, J, B, and G appeared among the first ten ranked subjects, but five subjects from the control group were also included. Subjects C, H, TM, A, E, and F did not achieve high places and Subject I did not carry out the delayed tasks.

Percentage retained over the week's delay was also calculated for each of the four tasks on which delayed performance was tested and these scores were ranked as before. Table 5.5 gives percentage retention on each of the delayed tasks, plus z scores calculated in the way explained in

TABLE 5.4

Mean Ranks and Overall Rank for 12 Subjects on Immediate Memory Tasks, Delayed Memory Tasks, and Retention

	Subject											
	A	B	C	D	E	F	G	H	I	J	JR	TM
Immediate												
Mean rank	31.3	16.6	11.9	9.9	17.4	17.5	5.7	15.2	8.1	24.0	7.4	12.6
Overall rank	37.0	12.5	6.0	4.0	15.0	16.0	1.0	11.0	3.0	24.0	2.0	7.0
Delayed												
Mean rank	27.9	8.0	17.1	3.4	19.1	21.0	9.1	27.3	–	7.0	2.4	21.3
Overall rank	29.0	6.0	12.0	2.0	16.0	19.0	7.0	28.0	–	5.0	1.0	20.0
Retention												
Mean rank	38.3	8.1	23.9	10.4	14.7[1]	24.6	15.6	23.3	–	3.5	4.5	21.5
Overall rank	32.5	5.0	23.0	6.0	–	25.0	12.0	20.5	–	1.0	3.0	16.0

[1] Based on three tasks only as subject scored 0 for both immediate and delayed recall of names to faces.

TABLE 5.5

Percentage Retained Over a Week and z Scores for the Difference between Observed and Predicted Scores on the Delayed Tests

	Subject								
	A	B	C	D	E	F	G	H	J
Story									
%	79	96	48	76	93	66	88	90	92
z	0.26	0.89	−2.20	−0.83	0.72	−1.24	0.27	0.92	0.56
Faces									
%	55	94	75	100	80	63	78	69	100
z	−2.46	0.42	−0.93	1.20	−0.52	−2.31	−0.79	−0.96	1.20
Names									
%	0	29	15	38	–	75	23	43	67
z	0	−0.22	−2.06	0.64	–	2.20	−1.22	1.44	2.31
Words									
%	38	62	60	75	43	23	48	9	75
z	0.89	1.13	1.54	1.90	−0.45	−2.21	−0.05	−2.98	1.90
Mean									
%	43	70	50	72	72[1]	57	59	53	84
z	−0.33	0.55	−0.91	0.73	-0.08[1]	−0.99	−0.45	−0.40	1.49

[1] Based on three tasks only as the subject scored 0 for immediate and delayed recall of names to faces.

Chapter 4. Table 5.4 also gives the results of ranking the percentages retained on the four tasks. These results indicate that Subjects J, JR, B, and D were the best performers in the expert group, but six subjects from the control group were in the first ten ranked places and Subjects C, H, TM, A, E, F, and G did not achieve high rankings. As indicated in Chapter 4, the data for retention of names were not strictly appropriate for regression analysis, since there was a preponderance of zero retention, but the general pattern of the results was not affected by omitting this score when computing the mean z score, so it has been retained in the calculation.

Clearly some control subjects did well (four were in the first ten ranked places on immediate performance, five on delayed and six on retention). For these subjects, z scores in relation to the control group are of course affected by their own scores, so are not directly comparable with those for the expert group. Table 5.6 gives the detailed scores for the three control subjects whose performance was at a high level on immediate performance, delayed performance, and retention, to enable comparison with results for the experts already presented. Table 5.7 gives mean ranks, overall ranks and z scores for these subjects. We will reserve comment on these results till later in the chapter.

Prime Ministers

Scores for Prime Ministers are given in Table 5.2. The experts in general scored slightly higher than the mean of the control group (5.11), but significantly so only in the case of Subject E (see Table 5.3). This was largely due to this subject's relatively low Mill Hill score, Mill Hill score being significantly related to memory for Prime Ministers.

Earliest Memory

Results for estimated age of earliest memory are shown in Table 5.9, later in the chapter, and did not differ significantly from the mean of the control group (3.39 years).

Earliest memories were also rated by the two experimenters on a five-point scale for the amount of detail included, visual and auditory imagery and references to taste, smell, touch and movement. Means were calculated from the ratings of the two experimenters and employed in the subsequent analysis. There was a high correlation between the mean rating of detail and the sum of the means of the other ratings (imagery and sensory references) with $r = 0.73$ ($P < .001$), indicating that the two measures were almost equivalent, so the single rating of detail was employed in further analysis. These ratings for the experts are shown in

TABLE 5.6
Scores on the Memory Tasks for Three Consistently Good
Performers From the Control Group

	Subject		
	33	36	45
Story			
immediate	86	107	98
delayed	91	89	95
Faces			
immediate	34	36	35
delayed	33	33	32
Names			
immediate	6.5	8	8
delayed	3.5	1	4
Words			
immediate			
correct	20	16	13
intrusions	0	0	1
delayed			
correct	14	7	7
intrusions	3	1	4
Telephone numbers			
immediate	17	24	30
Prime Ministers			
correct	5	8	9
intrusions	0	0	0
Pictures			
spatial	6.5	7.0	7.0
temporal	6.0	6.5	4.5
Snowflakes			
d'	1.49	1.05	1.34
Beta	1.77	1.45	2.46

Table 5.9. The mean for the control group was 3.34 (SD 1.41). Neither age nor Mill Hill score had any significant relation to the measure of detail. The rated detail for the experts was quite variable and the mean over these 10 subjects (3.5) was close to that of the control group. There was, however, a tendency for good memory performers to produce high scores, especially if high scorers not shown in Table 5.9 are also consid-

TABLE 5.7
Mean Rank, Overall Rank, and *z* Score on
Immediate Memory Tasks, Delayed Memory Tasks,
and Retention for Three Consistently Good
Performers from the Control Group

	Subject		
	33	*36*	*45*
Immediate			
Mean rank	14.2	10.6	14.1
Overall rank	8.5	5	8.5
Mean *z* score	0.62	1.03	0.78
Delayed			
Mean rank	4.5	11.4	6.9
Overall rank	3	9	4
Mean *z* score	1.67	0.81	1.22
Retention			
Mean rank	4.0	15.5	7.4
Overall rank	2	11	4
Mean *z* score	1.72	0.16	1.22

ered. JR scored 4.5, as did Subject 36 and TM scored 5. This measure is considered further in Chapter 6.

Number Matrix

Table 5.8 gives, for the subjects who attempted this task, the times to learn the 6×8 number matrix, to recall it and read it, and to recall selected parts of it in specified orders. The results on this task for VP, TE, and TM, which were referred to earlier, are presented in full here to enable comparisons. Eight of the ten subjects in the present sample (B, C, D, E, F, G, H, I) carried out this task and took an average of 378 seconds to learn the matrix, compared with 246 seconds for VP (Hunt & Love, 1972), 191.8 seconds for TE (Gordon et al., 1984), and 207 seconds for TM (Wilding & Valentine, 1994b). Several of these subjects did not attempt recall of the matrix a week later, so the data for this aspect of performance are very incomplete.

Recall took much longer than reading the matrix in all cases, suggesting that no subject was reading a visual image at recall. Recall of columns was also much slower than recall of rows, even for Column 1 which should be easy to locate visually if a visual image were being scanned. The pattern of recall for rows and columns in forward and

TABLE 5.8
Times (secs) Taken to Learn the Number Matrix Perfectly and in Recalling the Whole Matrix,
or Separate Rows and Columns as Indicated

	Subject										
	B	C	D	E	F	G	H	I	VP	TE	TM
Study time	308.0	160.0	721.0	540.0	660.0	376.0	72.0	185.0	246.0	191.8	207.0[2]
Recall whole	193.0	57.0	73.0	73.0	109.0	125.0	72.0	63.0	51.7	46.8	8.0
Read whole	13.0	16.0	22.0	15.6	13.6	13.0	17.0	9.8	19.4	18.2	27.0[2]
Row 6	13.0	4.0	8.0	17.2	12.4	19.0	7.0	11.0	5.7	4.0	1.0
Row 3	10.0	4.8	11.0	6.0	10.8	6.0	8.0	9.0	7.0	3.0	1.0
Column 4	50.0	36.8	46.0	25.5	60.0	66.0	102.0	42.0	26.7	49.6	31.5
Row 6 (backwards)	11.0	7.6	5.0	27.3	18.0	18.0	10.0	8.0	8.4	5.2	5.0
Column 1	55.0	30.2	21.0	26.2	32.0	32.0	24.6	30.0	10.6	23.2	39.0
Column 2 (upwards)	60.0	33.0	37.0	20.0	37.0	37.0	54.4	33.0	14.7	33.0	32.0
Diagonal from top left	–	36.2	53.0	7.4	56.4	57.0	142.0	21.4	–	–	–
Recall 1 week later (no. of items)	48	26	–	44	38	–	13	9[1]	–	–	47

[1] Recall seven weeks later; [2] One error in recall.

backward order is similar in nearly all cases, and shows no evidence that
any subject was reading off a visual image. In some cases backward recall
was faster than forward recall but the difference is not sufficiently striking
in any individual case to negate this conclusion.

Other Measures

Table 5.9 presents scores for each subject on the non-memory measures
that were taken. The distribution of Mill Hill vocabulary scores was
virtually bimodal, with one group of subjects falling at the very upper
end of the distribution (B, D, F, G, I) and the others at or somewhat
above the mean (TM, A, C, E, H, J—who was given the Junior version
of the test). This test was not given to JR.

All the subjects yielded very high scores on the Imaginal Thinking Scale
of the IDQ (Subject D did not complete this questionnaire). Scores on the
Verbal Thinking Scale of the same instrument were less uniformly high

TABLE 5.9
Age of Earliest Memory, Scores on Mill Hill Synonyms Test, and Imagery Measures

	Subject									
	A	*B*	*C*	*D*	*E*	*F*	*G*	*H*	*I*	*J*
Age (years) of earliest memory	3.0	2.5	3.0	3.0	2.5	4.0	2.5	2.0	5.0	4.0
Detail in earliest memory	2.5	4.5	2.0	4.5	2.5	3.0	4.5	3.0	3.5	4.5
Mill Hill percentile	69	96	69	99	66	95	95	50	90	50
Imaginal thinking	34	31	38	37	34	30	31	32	31	37
Verbal thinking	40	25	17	37	37	39	42	34	29	18
VVIQ (eyes open)	80	72	47	59	48	55	80	51	39	66

Norms: imaginal thinking, mean 18.4, SD 2.83; verbal thinking, mean 22.0, SD 3.59; VVIQ, mean 62.7, SD 11.76 (NB VVIQ scores from eyes open condition only have been reversed compared with the usual scoring method so that they range from 16 to 80, high scores indicating high imagery).

but Subjects A, D, E, F, G, H, I, and TM scored significantly above the norm. There is clearly no correlation between self-reported use of memory strategies and this score.

On the VVIQ, exceptionally vivid imagery was reported by Subjects A, B, G, J, and TM (no scores were available from JR). Again, there was no correlation with reported strategy use.

Individual Comments

The subjects were all asked after each task about any methods they had used to aid memory. Their individual results will now be described and discussed in the light of these comments.

Subject A.   The performance of this subject was modest, apart from recall of the story and of the names of Prime Ministers. Though this matched his emphasis that memory depended on motivation and interest in the material rather than some special ability, the results were somewhat disappointing in the light of his known achievements and his description of his abilities. Long-term retention was not impressive.

Subject B.   As was to be expected from this subject's description of his own abilities, he did especially well on tasks involving numbers. His immediate recall of telephone numbers was good and his delayed recall of these was better than that of all the other subjects except TM. His long-term retention of the matrix was particularly impressive, as he could recall it perfectly a week (and in fact two months) later, a feat matched by no other subject. He said that he used "brute force" on all the non-numerical tasks. He did quite well on the snow crystals, but refused even to attempt recall of Prime Ministers, saying he had no interest in this topic. Retention was also generally good.

This subject had been thinking about the operation of his own memory for several years and had many interesting observations to contribute. He said that normally he did not find a single exposure adequate to fix material firmly but needed two exposures or time to study the material. Of the present tasks, only the telephone numbers and the matrix met this requirement; coincidentally these both involved numbers, which were his favoured material, so his exceptional performance on these two tasks may have been due to either of these factors.

Given adequate time he said he was able to construct a memory representation which he could "see". He stated:

> I can 'see' the matrix in my 'mind's eye', but not in a photographic way. It is a little difficult to describe, but basically it is possible for me to see a few numbers at a time, in a 'window'. I can move the window around and new numbers appear. The nearest analogy I can think of is blind chess when the player may not 'see' all of the board at one time, but is 'aware' in some sense of the interrelationships of the pieces, and can focus on any part of the board that he or she desires.

More recently this subject has learned pi to 10,000 places and undertaken a test in which he was given a string of five digits from pi and required to supply the five preceding and five succeeding digits. He took 53 minutes to carry out 50 such tests, but 30 minutes of this time were occupied on just two of the problems, so the other 48 tests took him just 23 minutes.

Subject C. This subject relied on the method of loci, for which he had a variety of possible routes available (he avoids reusing a route for at least half an hour). His recall or recognition was always carried out very rapidly and performance was perfect on tasks amenable to his methods (faces, names, words, and telephone numbers, the last being learned perfectly after one exposure). When the method was not applicable he did less well. On the story, which he visualised taking place on a golf course, one of his practised routes, he performed adequately but lost concentration when he tried to apply his method to memorising a long African name. Similarly he tried, during the task itself, to invent a method of retaining the spatial and the temporal positions of the pictures perfectly. Not surprisingly, this interfered with his recall. Performance on the snow crystals was also respectable but not exceptional.

Delayed recall was modest on all tasks, though recall of the story was in fact further depressed because he did not attempt it until after four weeks away on holiday. The other delayed tests were done after about one and a half weeks' delay.

Subject D. Without employing any practised techniques, this subject performed very well on the story, names, and spatial and temporal recall of pictures. Unfortunately it was not possible to score initial performance on the story exactly, as the recording apparatus failed and we had to estimate the score (by this stage we had a great deal of experience in scoring other recalls of the same story). This subject used a modest aid in recalling names to faces, thinking of a feature that began with the same letter as the name, but said that she normally found the task of remembering names an easy one without any such aid, as a variety of information would normally be available about the person. Retention over a week was generally good (no exact estimate was of course possible in the case of the story).

Subject E. This subject did best on face recognition and word recall, but only modestly otherwise. Delayed recall of the matrix was at a high level. Matrix learning was the only task for which this subject employed a technique. This was to divide the figures into 2×2 squares and find some pattern in the four numbers contained in the miniature matrix, such as both diagonals adding to 10. He claimed that after more rehearsal he could eventually "see" an image of the matrix. Retention was not exceptional.

Subject F. used a variety of not very systematic methods, such as exaggerating features of faces and creating an association to the names, but found presentation was too fast to do this efficiently. Nevertheless, overall performance was good and he was the only subject to achieve perfect performance in recalling both the spatial and the temporal positions of the pictures. To do this he used a visual image for the former attribute and a story for the latter. Retention was not impressive.

Subject G. achieved the best overall performance (note again that this subject had highly developed techniques but also claimed to have an excellent natural memory). He used visualisation to aid recall of the story, but no special method for memorising the faces. To learn names to faces he looked for distinctive features or a similarity to someone he already knew if the name was the same as that of an acquaintance. He used the method of loci to retain the words. The telephone numbers and the matrix numbers were converted to words, using the set of associations to playing cards that he had memorised. The words for each row were combined into a sentence and the sentences stored in order using the method of loci. The spatial order of the pictures was retained by linking the pictures to a set of conceptual pegs and the temporal order was retained by linking items in a chain of associations. For each snowflake pattern he tried to find a key feature.

It is likely that the delayed scores underestimate retention ability of this subject because he practised a method of deliberately forgetting unwanted material. He claimed that, if he had been given warning of a further test, he would have reviewed the material and that this would have ensured virtually perfect retention. "By reviewing anything I may need in future a couple of times, I can commit it to long-term memory ... whereas I actually visualise dissolving and disappearing those things that I won't need again." Both S (Luria, 1975) and Leslie Welch (Hunter, 1990) are reported to have used similar methods. Despite this deliberate forgetting, Subject G's retention was somewhat above average.

Subject H. used his practised methods for faces, names (though not with outstanding success in this case), words, telephone numbers, and the number matrix, which he learned in just over one minute, 88 seconds faster than any other subject. He looked for distinctive features when memorising faces or recalled persons he knew who looked similar to the presented face. When learning names to faces he concocted an association to the name. Stratford elicited an image of a Shakespearian actor, Rowan an image of a boat. He then distorted the image of the face to match this association. To learn the words, he used a form of digit–letter alphabet. The numbers 1 to 25 were first connected to letters and these letters to words: 1—ta(r), 2—nay, 3—may, and so on. These words were linked to the words presented in order of presentation. Six-digit phone numbers were divided into two groups of three digits and each group was converted into a word through the digit–letter alphabet and then linked to the names, the latter being modified in a way that would produce a vivid association. For example, Stelman was modified to Stillman, which was associated with real ale. He looked for meaningful shapes in the snow crystals, such as cat's ears or a lace mat. His performance on the tasks not suited to the techniques was not good, that on the story being very poor, as was delayed recall. The subject attributed the poor retention to "the fact that I have been memorising many things since, thereby dulling the images from last week".

Subject I. used pegwords, the digit–letter alphabet, selection and exaggeration of features of faces, these methods producing a good all-round performance. However, recall of the story, which he said he turned into a film, was also impressive, implying that the subject's assertion that he had a "terrible" memory should be taken with some scepticism. Alternatively, practice with techniques may have improved memory in general. Due to other commitments, this subject was unable to carry out the delayed recall until seven weeks after the original session; not surprisingly very little had been retained.

Subject J. This 13-year old boy had attempted the Memoriad tasks while in the audience and found he could do several of them very well. He did not perform exceptionally well on our tasks, but his results were respectable compared with the adults. His retention after a week, however, was outstanding, being comparable to that of JR discussed in the previous chapter. Since both these subjects were teenagers, however, more data are needed to determine whether such a high level of retention is characteristic of younger subjects in general. The only other subject who has shown this level of retention was ED, aged 67, in the sample contacted by radio and discussed in Chapter 4, so this ability is not restricted to teenagers.

DISCUSSION

The implications of these results for the questions about superior memory performance in Chapter 1 will be considered in detail in Chapter 7. The present discussion will take a more limited view of the results. We will look at the levels and patterns of performance achieved by the memory experts, differences and relations between the immediate and delayed memory performance, and also the results of the measures of verbal and imagery ability. Finally, the issue of the contribution of strategic methods and natural ability to memory performance will be addressed.

The first question concerns the memory performance of these "expert" subjects. Were they in fact superior to the general population and, if so, to what extent? In several cases the answer is clearly a positive one for the immediate tasks. Including JR and TM in this assessment, Subjects G, JR, I, C, TM, H, and D all attained mean ranks in the top 10 places out of 43 and achieved the best mean z scores (all over 1.0 and more than 2½ standard deviations above the expected mean). It should be noted that the mean ranks and mean z scores produce slightly different overall rankings. Measured by mean rank, three control subjects also fell in the top 10 places, but only one of these (Subject 36) achieved a mean z score of more than 1.00. Thus the best performers certainly came from the group which claimed to possess superior memory, though it is equally true that several of the other claimants failed to live up to their reputation (Subjects A, B, E, F, J). Furthermore, several of the best performers were demonstrating a very high level of performance indeed. Subject G's mean z score was 4.6 standard deviations above the expected mean ($P <$ .0001) and JR, I, C, and TM all produced mean z scores more than three standard deviations above the expected mean ($P < .01$).

This picture changes considerably when delayed scores are considered. Subjects G, JR, and D still produced mean ranks in the top ten places, as did Subjects B and J (Subject I did not carry out the delayed tasks), but five of the control subjects were ranked in the top ten places. The mean z scores yield the same picture. The best performance was that of JR (7.52 standard deviations above the expected mean), control Subject 33 (3.34), Subject D (3.30), control Subject 45 (2.44), and Subject J (2.26). No other subject achieved a mean z score more than two standard deviations above the expected mean.

Not unexpectedly a similar pattern emerges from examination of the proportion retained. By rank Subjects J (first), JR (third), B (fifth), and D (sixth) figured in the top ten places but the other six places were all occupied by subjects from the control group, including Subjects 33 and 45 again, ranked second and fourth. Subject G was in twelfth position. It will be recalled that he practised deliberate forgetting, but he nevertheless achieved a high level of delayed recall from an initially exceptional level of performance. Subject J, it should be noted, was only 13 years' old, and his initial scores may under-represent his ability; equally, his high level of delayed recall and retention may be age-related, as no norms were available for his age group.

Mean z scores for retention (derived as explained earlier) produced a slightly different pattern and showed that only some of these subjects performed impressively on this more refined measure. Subject J scored 2.98 standard deviations above the expected mean on the four tasks, JR 7.04, Subject D only 1.46, Subject 33 scored 3.44, and Subject 45 was 2.44 standard deviations above the expected mean. Subject G scored below the expected mean (−0.9 standard deviations).

There is, therefore, evidence that on the immediate memory tasks several subjects, nearly all from the expert group, were performing at a high level across a considerable range of tasks. However, examination of Table 5.2, together with the comments made by the subjects, indicates that there was also considerable variability in performance by individual subjects across tasks. To some extent this was due to variation in task difficulty. The face recognition task was too easy (eight of the control group achieved the maximum score). Immediate memory for names to faces produced around 40% correct responses but delayed recall in the control group was virtually zero, as was delayed recall of telephone numbers in response to names (in fact, the task was discontinued because almost every subject found it impossible). However, these two tasks, by their very difficulty, enabled demonstration of very high superiority by a few subjects. Several subjects, some but not all using strategies, achieved perfect recall of names to faces on the immediate test and JR achieved a remarkable score of 12/13 correct on delayed recall, representing no forgetting, yet described no strategy. TM recalled 35/36 telephone digits at delayed recall, having used a strategy, and Subject B recalled 24/36 digits in the same task without describing a strategy.

General variation in task difficulty, however, does not explain all the pronounced variation across tasks within individual subjects. Subject H, for example, recognised faces and recalled telephone numbers perfectly yet, like TM, recalled the story very poorly, and only performed at a moderate level on the pictures. Subject C was perfect on faces, names, words, and telephone numbers, yet only moderate on pictures and snow crystals. JR was good at everything except the telephone numbers. Subject B performed at a reasonably good level on most tasks. He was weak on faces and pictures, but was perfect on immediate recall of the telephone numbers and very good at delayed recall of these. Likewise, his delayed recall of the number matrix was perfect. These variations in the pattern of strengths and weaknesses would seem to rule out any explanation in terms of general differences in task difficulty.

What are the implications of such variations within and between subjects? One possibility is that subjects were able to deploy techniques appropriate to only some tasks. Use of techniques and the implications of such use will be considered in more detail in Chapter 7, where it will be argued that such an explanation does account for many differences in the level of performance between tasks in the case of some subjects. Subjects C, G, H, and TM (and to a lesser extent Subject I) had powerful techniques available for learning faces, names, words, and numbers, demonstrating perfect or nearly perfect immediate performance on almost all these tasks, but they performed less well on other tasks.

A second possibility is that long experience with some types of material enabled familiar recoding devices to be activated. Subject B was especially familiar with, and interested in, numbers and demonstrated particularly good performance with these. However, he claimed that this was also due to a natural ability, though the present data do not enable any obvious test between these possibilities. JR, on the other hand, was weak in memorising numbers compared with her performance on other types of material.

A third possibility is that differences between tasks reflect the operation of distinct memory systems. This could be true for numbers, but no other consistent pattern of strengths and weaknesses is apparent to suggest such a conclusion (see Chapter 7). The tasks employed were not ideally suited for testing such an hypothesis, omitting as they do any tests of spatial ability, motor memory, musical memory, etc. The most that can be said is that the evidence presented for general superiority over a range of tasks is highly suggestive of some general memory ability. It would be desirable in future studies to widen the choice of tasks to include more from non-visual modalities and non-verbal materials and to test systematically the importance of retrieval in superior performance.

However, the data do confirm the tentative indication from the case of ED discussed in Chapter 4 that superior long-term retention may depend on different mechanisms from those determining the initial level of recall. Presumably the latter depends to a large extent on the efficiency of the initial encoding process. While the expert subjects in this sample provided nearly all the best overall performances on the immediate memory tests (filling the first seven places, as measured by mean z score), only three of these subjects showed outstanding delayed recall and retention. Two control subjects demonstrated high levels of performance on the latter measures, as did two of the expert subjects who had not been among the top performers on immediate testing. One notable fact, to be discussed later in more detail, is that subjects who depended heavily on memory strategies tended to perform much less impressively on delayed recall and retention. The high performance of some of the control subjects on delayed recall and retention also implies that strategic factors were not important, as these subjects did not report that they were employing special strategies.

Adequate data for a thorough examination of these issues requires large samples and factor analysis to explore the independence of initial memory and retention. A pilot study using the present data is reported in the next chapter. Meanwhile it may be hypothesised that outstanding memory ability requires both superior initial encoding and superior long-term retention. The subjects in our sample who demonstrate such a combination most clearly are JR, D, and probably G (given that his long-term retention was depressed by deliberate forgetting, but still at a respectable level). Of the subjects discussed earlier, S, VP, Aitken, and TE all seem to have possessed both these characteristics.

STRATEGISTS VS. NATURALS

The previous discussion has referred from time to time to the self-reports of subjects about their method for memorising material, or in some cases to the absence of a method. Data obtained from self-reports are, however, notoriously suspect as the basis for firm conclusions about behaviour and more objective indices are desirable to identify important individual differences between subjects in their memorising strategies. It is apparent from the variety of cases of superior memory discussed in the preceding chapters that an adequate understanding cannot be based on any single explanatory factor. The case against Ericsson's skilled memory theory as a complete explanation of superior performance has been presented in detail already in Chapters 2 and 3. However, if we wish to argue for a number of different types of memory superiority, a satisfactory taxonomy will need to be developed, together with objective methods of assigning subjects to the different hypothesised types.

Given that the present study included a sizeable sample of superior performers, an opportunity is presented to take the first steps along this path. An initial goal can be to devise methods of discriminating memory superiority based on strategic methods from superiority for which no such explanation is tenable. Some possible criteria are as follows.

Generality of Superior Performance. Superior performance on a limited range of tasks can be due either to exercise of strategies only applicable to tasks with specific features, special experience with certain types of material, or division of memory into independent modular systems. A decision between these possibilities has to be based on factors like consistency between self-reported strategies and features of performance, such as the types of error made. This would support a strategy-based taxonomy. Alternatively, agreement between the grouping of the tasks that produce superior performance and groupings established on other grounds, such as patterns of loss after brain damage, would suggest differences in underlying memory systems.

Superior performance over a wider range of tasks (but note the difficulty at this stage of defining what is a wide or limited range of tasks) would suggest both that some common process underlies all or most memory performance and that individual variation in the efficiency of this process can be demonstrated.

Thus, if tasks can be differentiated into those readily amenable to the application of memory strategies and those less amenable, self-declared strategists should show a greater difference in performance between strategic and non-strategic tasks than naturals. Subjects with natural memory ability, on the other hand, should show superiority on both types of task; it is likely, but not certain, that they will perform less well than strategists on the strategic tasks but better than strategists on the non-strategic tasks.

Retention. Claims of natural memory superiority must be based largely on ability to retain everyday information better than the average person. This will be most dramatically demonstrated by long-term retention without use of special rehearsal or other methods. Some examples have been quoted above. Hence, it is suggested that long-term retention without expectation of a delayed test will be superior in subjects possessing natural memory superiority.

Early Awareness of Superior Memory. Natural memory superiority is likely to be apparent at an early age, whereas acquisition of memory techniques can begin at any point in life and is likely to attract teenage or older individuals.

Familial Ability. Natural memory ability should depend on some aspect of genetic endowment, so is likely to run in families. However, correlations between parents and children might equally be due to specific aspects of upbringing, so this form of evidence could not be decisive.

Given that almost every subject faced with a memory task will call on experience to determine the best way of tackling it, the possibility of distinguishing users of strategies from non-users, or "basic" memory ability from strategically supported remembering, may be questioned. It is not true, however, that subjects generally come to the laboratory test of memory with a special battery of memory methods, which they have developed with much labour and regular practice. Only the dedicated student of mnemonics does this. The basis of our distinction, therefore, was not whether subjects just tried to memorise or used some aid such as a story or first letter mnemonic, but whether or not they had deliberately learned a set of methods and practised them, and had them immediately available. Of the best eight performers on the immediate tasks identified earlier by mean z score (seven experts and one control subject), four were habitual users of mnemonic methods (TM, C, G, H) and three were not (JR, D, Subject 36). Subject I was difficult to assign firmly to one group or the other, though probably falling into the strategic group. (Including him made minimal difference to the comparisons described later.) We wanted to know whether the criteria proposed would discriminate between these two groups previously differentiated on the basis of self-reported use of practised mnemonic methods.

Strategic vs. Non-strategic Tasks

In order to employ this criterion, a decision had to be made as to which tasks were amenable to strategies and which were not. By examination of the subjects' comments obtained during the experimental sessions about how they had performed each task, it was relatively easy to decide which tasks attracted the most detailed and consistent accounts of strategic methods prepared beforehand. Well-established methods (with some variations on general themes) are available for memorising the faces, names, words, and telephone numbers. Most of these have been outlined already. Basically, they all depend on association and imagery. Faces can be linked to names by finding an association between the name, modified if necessary, and a distinctive feature of the face. Faces alone can be remembered by forming an association to a distinctive and possibly exaggerated feature. Words can be recalled by linking them into a story, constructing a composite image in which they interact, or linking them to a previously learned peg system. The rhyme "One is a bun, two is a shoe", etc. is one example; the method of loci in which items are placed along a known route is another. Numbers likewise can be memorised using pre-learned systems; those used by TE and TM described earlier are examples.

Though some subjects attempted to apply similar methods to parts of the story, no single method was used widely or consistently. Devising methods to aid memorisation of the spatial and temporal ordering of the pictures and of the snow crystals presented problems because of the unfamiliarity and complexity of the material. Subjects tried to fall back on established methods but rarely managed to "streamline" these in time to apply them successfully to the novel tasks. Most said, however, that they would be able to do this if given a second chance.

Figure 5.1 shows the mean z scores for the strategic and non-strategic tasks for the two groups of subjects. As predicted, strategists performed at a high level on "strategic" tasks and at a level close to average on "non-strategic" tasks; naturals did equally well and better than average on both types of task, surpassing strategists on the non-strategic tasks but doing worse than strategists on the strategic tasks. The interaction between type of task and group was significant ($F(1, 5) = 34.7$, $P = .002$).

Retention

Table 5.5 and the subsequent comments have indicated already that naturals showed much better retention than the strategists. The average percentage retention scores were 83 and 53 and the mean z scores were 1.69 and -0.46 respectively ($t = 2.71$, $P < .005$). However, a number of qualifications should be made. Of the strategists, Subject C did not recall the story until four weeks after the initial presentation, Subject G employed deliberate forgetting (though in fact achieving the best retention in the group of strategists), and Subject H claimed to have suffered interference from intervening public memory demonstrations. On the other

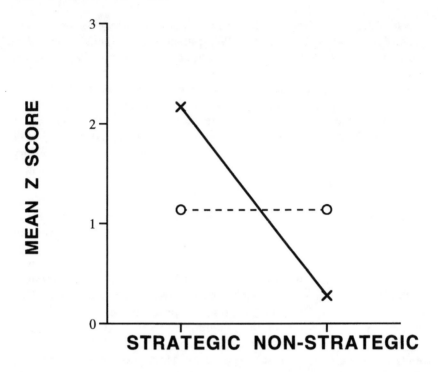

Fig. 5.1.   Mean *z* score for immediate memory for strategists (solid line and crosses) and naturals (dashed line and circles) on strategic and non-strategic tasks.

hand, three of the four tasks on which delayed performance was measured were strategic tasks on which the four strategists had achieved, at initial testing, an average of 100% correct on faces, 84% correct on names, and 97% correct on words, compared with 97%, 85%, and 72% respectively in the case of the three naturals. Delayed recall produced 76%, 15%, and 48% correct responses respectively for the three tasks in the case of the strategists, compared with 94%, 46%, and 53% for the naturals. The other delayed recall task was the story, on which the strategists scored 31% and 21% correct for immediate and delayed recall, while the naturals scored 58% and 47% correct.

Though the sample in each group is very small, additional evidence can be cited in support of the difference apparent in these comparisons. The only strategist in the first 10 ranked places on delayed recall was Subject G, who claimed to have a very good natural memory. Two subjects from the expert group, who did not show high ranked performance on the immediate tests, were ranked fifth and sixth on delayed recall; both were non-strategists (Subjects B and J). Five control subjects (presumably naturals, though only one was explicitly questioned about methods) appeared among the first ten places on delayed recall.

Early Awareness

Two of the naturals and two of the strategists claimed early awareness of superior memory ability. This criterion, therefore, did not discriminate between the groups.

Relatives

All the naturals cited a near relative with an excellent memory, but only two of the four strategists did so. This is no more than suggestive.

Comparisons between Strategists and Naturals on Other Measures

An attempt was made to compare strategists and naturals on recall of the number matrix, it being hypothesised that the strategists would be superior at this task. However, two of the three naturals in the comparisons did not complete learning of the matrix (JR and Subject 36). Those subjects who did learn the matrix were classified as strategists or non-strategists according to their self-report (see Table 5.1). Mean time to learn and recall the matrix was faster in the strategists (264 seconds to learn and 69 seconds to recall on average) but these did not differ significantly from the corresponding times for the naturals (523 and 113 seconds). Nor were there any significant differences between the groups in times to recall specified rows and columns.

No significant differences between groups emerged in relation to scores on IDQ, VVIQ, or Mill Hill vocabulary.

CONCLUSIONS

This study has demonstrated that individuals can be identified who show superior memory performance over a range of tasks and that such subjects do not always report the use of special strategies. Differences between subjects reporting use of such strategies and those who do not can be demonstrated in the pattern of their performance. Subjects who employ strategies demonstrate superior performance on tasks amenable to the strategies, but their performance is less impressive on tasks to which strategies are not easily applicable. Non-strategists or "naturals" do not perform as well as strategists on the strategic tasks, but show a less striking but more consistent superiority over the whole range of tasks. They also show better retention on an unexpected delayed test.

In the next chapter a pilot study is reported in which data from all subjects who did not admit to using strategies were subjected to a factor analysis to discover whether a general memory factor could be identified and whether immediate memory and retention ability would emerge as separate factors.

6

General Memory Ability and Forgetting—Evidence from the Group Data

Chapter 5 focused on a comparison of the results of subjects believed to possess superior memory ability with the control group, as befits the main objectives of this book. However, some of the questions originally posed can also be approached by considering the body of data as a whole. Issues such as whether a general memory ability can be identified or whether several separate memory abilities exist, whether a retention process can be identified that is distinct from initial coding, relations between memory ability as demonstrated in laboratory tasks and aspects of autobiographical memory, and relations between memory ability and other aspects of cognitive ability, can all be investigated by examining intercorrelations in the data collected during the course of the series of studies described earlier.

This chapter, therefore, while not directly related to the theme of superior memory, will provide an extensive footnote to some of these central issues before a final evaluation of the evidence is attempted in Chapter 7.

It would, however, be unjustified simply to amalgamate the data from all the subjects who have figured in Chapters 4 and 5. It has been argued in Chapter 5 that subjects who employ highly practised strategies on appropriate tasks produce a different pattern of results from subjects who do not employ such strategies. Consequently TM (Chapter 4) and Subjects C, G, H, and I from the Memoriad sample (Chapter 5) should be excluded from a sample designed to reflect normal variation in performance, and Subject J, being an outlier on the age dimension, should probably also be excluded. The 10 subjects recruited following a radio broadcast, though they claimed superior memory ability, did not clearly demonstrate it and none of them admitted to using well-practised mnemonic methods (see Chapter 4). Consequently there is no strong reason for excluding this group and the same applies to JR (Chapter 4) and Subjects A, B, D, E, and F from the Memoriad sample (Chapter 5). Together with the 31 subjects in the Control group, this produces a total sample of 47 subjects (13 males and 34 females) with an age range from 17 to 70 years.

Distributions of variables were inspected for normality and, as already reported, two were found to be distributed in a markedly non-normal manner. Nine subjects achieved the maximum score on immediate face recognition, and the distribution of scores was markedly skewed negatively, so scores were reduced to three categories: 22–29 (10 subjects), 30–35 (28 subjects), and 36 (9 subjects). In recalling names to faces after a week, 24 subjects achieved a score of zero; no transformation could compensate for this pattern of results and consequently the corresponding retention score was omitted from further consideration. Also one subject with an extreme outlying score (14 years) on the age of earliest memory was excluded from the calculations involving this variable.

Table 6.1 gives the correlations between seven immediate memory scores (story, faces, names, words, telephone numbers, spatio-temporal positions of pictures, snow crystals, plus recall of Prime Ministers), three retention scores (story, faces and words), age, age of earliest memory, amount of detail in earliest memory, and Mill Hill vocabulary score. The following points may be noted.

1. Scores on names, words, telephone numbers, pictures, and snow crystals are positively and significantly intercorrelated ($r \geqslant 0.28$, $P < .05$ by a one-tailed test in all cases and at a more impressive level of significance in most cases). Performance on these tasks also declined significantly with age. Apart from snow crystals ($r = -0.22$, $P = .07$ by a one-tailed test), all the scores were correlated significantly with age ($r \geqslant -0.36$, $P < .01$ by a one-tailed test).

    Memory for a story and memory for faces were less consistently related to the other measures and the correlations were weaker, even where they were significant. There was thus some evidence for a general memory factor, but also a suggestion that some memory tasks may involve either fewer, more, or different processes.
2. Of the three retention scores, retention of words correlated with all the immediate memory scores, strongly in all cases except memory for a story, and with the other two retention scores. The latter two

TABLE 6.1
Intercorrelations of the Variables

	2	3	4	5	6	7	8	9	10	11	12	13	14	15
1. Story	0.25	0.36	0.25	0.27	0.07	0.23	0.32	0.25	0.03	0.31	-0.23	-0.29	0.33	0.32
2. Faces		0.35	0.35	0.04	-0.05	0.23	0.26	0.26	0.02	0.44	-0.36	-0.06	0.01	-0.11
3. Names			0.44	0.50	-0.30	0.49	0.42	0.16	0.29	0.57	-0.41	-0.02	0.43	0.30
4. Words				0.46	-0.36	0.56	0.41	0.27	0.25	0.57	-0.65	0.00	0.21	0.09
5. Telephone numbers					0.02	0.38	0.28	0.28	0.25	0.48	-0.55	-0.17	0.31	0.17
6. Prime Ministers						-0.19	-0.13	0.06	-0.09	-0.40	0.26	-0.25	-0.19	0.25
7. Pictures							0.20	0.16	-0.04	0.48	-0.52	0.25	0.18	0.01
8. Snow crystals								0.11	0.06	0.41	-0.22	-0.09	0.36	0.21
9. Story retention									0.15	0.54	-0.16	0.05	0.00	-0.02
10. Faces retention										0.38	-0.26	-0.13	0.13	0.30
11. Words retention											-0.62	0.24	0.17	-0.04
12. Age												0.01	-0.12	0.07
13. Age of earliest memory													-0.13	-0.12
14. Detail in earliest memory														0.27
15. Mill Hill vocabulary														

$r(0.05) = 0.29$; $r(0.01) = 0.37$; $r(0.001) = 0.46$ (two-tailed tests).

scores were correlated with only a few of the immediate memory scores and these correlations were relatively weak. There was also only a low correlation between retention of a story and of faces. There was, therefore, a suggestion that one retention process, reflected in retention of words, was closely related to initial encoding ability. This was further supported by the strong correlation between retention of words and age. However, one or more other retention processes may also exist that are reflected in the retention of a story and of faces and are not closely related to age.

3. Memory for the names of Prime Ministers correlated positively but weakly with age ($r = 0.27$, $P = .08$) implying that those with direct experience of Premiers remember their names better. This variable was also related negatively to word retention and memory for names and words. Clearly it measures something quite different from the other memory tasks employed in this study.

4. Reported age of earliest memory correlated negatively with memory for a story, so the later the early memory the worse the story recall.

5. Rated detail in earliest memory was significantly related to a number of the other scores (memory for the story, names, telephone numbers, and snow crystals). Subjects giving more detail generally scored higher on the memory tasks.

6. Mill Hill vocabulary score is presumably a measure of memory for words and their meanings. It was, however, unrelated to most of the memory scores, only the correlations with story recall and name recall proving significant, though at a modest level in both cases ($P < .05$ on a one-tailed test). The Mill Hill score also correlated modestly with retention of faces, higher Mill Hill score being related to better retention ($P = .05$ by a one-tailed test).

FACTOR ANALYSIS

The obvious procedure to discover whether a single memory factor can be identified in these data and the relation of such a factor to retention, age, age of earliest memory, amount of detail in earliest memory, and Mill Hill score, was to carry out a factor analysis. However, this presented some problems. Due to the relatively small number of cases, it was not possible to include all the measures in a single factor analysis (the recommended ratio of cases to measures is at least 5:1). Furthermore, no Mill Hill scores were taken from the subjects employed in the earlier studies. Therefore, only the seven immediate memory scores (story, faces, names, words, telephone numbers, spatio-temporal positions of pictures, and snow crystals) and

TABLE 6.2
Results of the Maximum Likelihood Factor Analysis

	Factor 1	Factor 2	Factor 3
Eigen value	1.93	0.96	2.48
Percentage of variance	19.30	9.60	24.80
Loadings ($\geqslant$ 0.40)			
Story	0.40		
Faces	0.43		
Names	0.72		
Words	0.68		
Telephone numbers	0.53		
Pictures	0.69		
Snow crystals	0.53		
Story retention		0.98	
Face retention			0.99
Word retention	0.69	0.41	
Correlation of factors with			
Age	−0.68**	−0.11	−0.22
Age of earliest memory	0.07	−0.05	−0.09
Detail in earliest memory	0.40*	−0.02	0.08
Mill Hill vocabulary	0.11	−0.06	0.30

*$P < 0.01$; **$P < 0.001$.

the three retention scores (story, faces, and words) were submitted to a Maximum Likelihood Factor analysis with Varimax rotation (a number of alternative methods were found to produce essentially the same pattern of results). This procedure yielded three factors and this conclusion was supported by the scree plot. Details of these factors are given in Table 6.2. Correlations of the factors with age, age of earliest memory, detail in earliest memory, and Mill Hill score are also given in the table (none of the factors showed any relation to recall of the names of Prime Ministers).

The first factor comprised all the immediate memory scores, plus retention of words. It was also highly age dependent. Clearly this is the general memory factor which was apparent in the pattern of correlations discussed previously. It was also positively related to the amount of detail in the earliest memory. To check that the last relation was independent of the age of the earliest memory, a regression analysis was carried out with detail in the earliest memory as the dependent variable and age, age of earliest memory and Factor 1 as the independent variables. Factor 1 was significantly related to detail in earliest memory (t = 3.00, P < .01) but neither age of earliest memory (t = −0.73) nor age (t = 1.35) showed any significant relation to the amount of detail. Thus subjects scoring high on Factor 1 produced more detail in their earliest memory. It was gratifying to find such a relation between a measure of "real-life" memory and a laboratory task measure.

The second factor consisted of retention of the story and of words. It was not correlated with age. The third factor was retention of faces and showed sizeable but non-significant correlations with age and Mill Hill score.

None of the three factors had any significant relation to Mill Hill vocabulary score, which was somewhat surprising as the latter would seem to reflect long-term memory for words. However, this finding supports the general picture of minimal relationships between memory ability (other than measures of Working Memory and short-term serial memory) and measures of intelligence. Nor did any factor correlate with memory for Prime Ministers.

While these results demonstrate reasonably clearly the existence of a general memory ability displayed in Factor 1, they do not support the existence of a single retention process. Factors 2 and 3 both represent retention processes but word retention loads on both Factor 1 and Factor 2, and Factor 3 reflects only one score, face retention. This was the only delayed test involving recognition and it is possible that this is the reason for its separation from Factor 2; both the tasks loading on the latter required retrieval. Alternatively, the tendency toward a ceiling effect on the immediate face recognition scores may have meant that the retention scores on this task are not fully representative of the full range of performance. Since only three retention scores were available for the Factor Analysis, there is a need for caution in interpreting the results. Nevertheless, they do support a separation of immediate memory performance, perhaps dependent largely on efficiency of encoding, from retention, which may reflect retrieval efficiency as well as storage.

Age affected performance on the immediate memory tests, which it is suggested reflects largely encoding efficiency, but was not significantly related to either of the retention factors. Rabbitt (1993a, pp. 225–226) has reported other evidence demonstrating a similar absence of relation between age and forgetting. He also reports a study by Yang Qian (Rabbitt, 1993b, p. 424), which carefully matched initial levels of recall and time before delayed recall in younger and older subjects. This did show an effect of age on retention (see Chapter 3). It seems likely that retention is less sensitive to age effects than encoding and short-term recall.

CONCLUSIONS

This analysis has provided support for the existence of a general memory factor underlying performance on a range of immediate memory tasks and also suggests that retention may depend on processes that are distinct from those responsible for immediate memory. Age was primarily related to immediate memory performance but not to retention. Subjects who demonstrated better immediate memory also reported more detail in their earliest memories, further supporting the view that stable pervading individual differences in memory can be identified. It is suggested that this factor reflects primarily the efficiency of encoding processes.

7

Conclusions

It is now time to look back over the evidence described in the preceding pages and decide what conclusions can be drawn in relation to the questions raised in Chapter 1.

SPECIFICITY OF SUPERIOR MEMORY AND REASONS FOR SUCH SPECIFICITY

Chapter 3 discussed the evidence for modularity in memory, that is to say distinct processing systems responsible for different types of memory or for processing different types of material. It was argued that such evidence does not preclude the possibility that some processes are common to memory performance over a range of different tasks. If separate modular systems do exist, memory superiority specific to one or more of these systems should sometimes occur. Does the evidence we have described include any such cases and can other possible reasons for memory superiority of a specific type be excluded?

Limited applicability of a strategy (or limited ability to apply it) may be one cause of apparent specificity in memory superiority. In many of the cases that have been described in Chapter 2, superior performance seems to have been restricted to a small number of similar tasks. The majority of examples are numerical. Inaudi, Diamandi, and Finkelstein are the clearest examples of superior performance restricted to numerical material. Somewhat less restricted examples are TM and some of the subjects described in Chapter 5. In these cases specific superiority was due to application of a limited strategy, but this is not always the case, nor is such specificity always restricted to numerical material. Rajan and Bubbles P demonstrated memory ability solely or almost solely with numerical material but neither appears to have depended on a strategy. Our Subject B (Chapter 5) also showed better performance with numerical than with other material, but his performance was less striking than that of Rajan and Bubbles P. Examples of specific ability with other material have also been noted: Gummerman and Gray's (1971) subject performed well only on recall of pictures; Stromeyer and Psotka's (1970) subject was tested only on ability to fuse stereograms separated in time; CJ (Novoa et al., 1988) was especially good at languages; and the autistic subjects described in Chapter 2 showed different but limited areas of expertise (e.g. routes, music, physical features).

Even though it seems unlikely that these restricted areas of expertise were due to employment of specific pre-learned strategies, they may have been due to intense interest in and exposure to numerical (or other) material, resulting in extensive knowledge and practice. This appears to have been the basis of Aitken's expertise with numbers, which enabled him to represent them as meaningful entities, though this does not explain all his abilities, for example his retention of verbal material over many years. Moreover, there is no evidence that Rajan or Bubbles P was adopting any such method. Likewise CJ's ability to learn languages, though certainly facilitated by general linguistic knowledge gained from languages he had already learned, appears to have had some innate component. Whether the memory abilities of the autistic subjects in specific areas were dependent on pre-existing biases in ability or to intense concentration over a prolonged period is virtually insoluble.

We can conclude from these cases that there are a few cases of specific abilities (and not the same abilities in all cases) that are unlikely to be due to either pre-learned specific strategies or intense exposure to the material. The number of such cases, however, is small and the abilities they demonstrate vary markedly.

There is no unequivocal pattern of expertise across the cases we have examined that matches hypothesised distinct modular information-processing systems in the brain. However, there is some similarity between different individuals, mainly manifest in specific ability with numerical material. The distinction that has been made most widely in theories of cognitive abilities is that between sequential verbal processes and visuo-spatial processes. Numerical processing has also been suggested as a candidate for a separate subordinate modular system. Hence, superiority in numerical memory might reflect the superior operation of this modular system, superior language learning might reflect the operation of the sequential verbal system, and superior memory for pictures might depend on the visuo-spatial system. However, it is unclear in the last case why superior performance was apparent in only very limited tasks in the cases which have been cited (Gummerman & Gray, 1971; Stromeyer & Psotka, 1970; possibly Coltheart & Glick, 1974). Also the available evidence does not completely match the hypothesised division between different types of processing. Rajan demonstrated increased span for letters as well as numbers and Bubbles P was good with playing cards as well as numbers. These results could indicate superiority of the sequential verbal system, but neither of these subjects showed unusual facility with all other verbal tasks.

Rajan demonstrated rather poor ability in remembering spatial locations, perhaps implying some form of trade-off between his exceptional skill with numbers and his visuo-spatial ability. CJ may have had some weakness in spatial processing, combined with his exceptional skill in language processing. However, such a trade-off is certainly not the general rule, since subjects as different as Aitken and the three autistic subjects demonstrated unusual ability in tasks involving both verbal and spatial material. Aitken was good at many memory tasks, Elly with routes, positions of objects, words, and numbers, Paul with routes and music, and JD with routes, music, and picture locations.

A major problem in trying to derive clear interpretations and conclusions is that the supposed modular divisions in information processing are far from clear. Precisely what is included in sequential/verbal processing or visuo-spatial processing is not immediately obvious. More specific modules have been proposed on the basis of clinical evidence of specific impairments in recognising faces, locations, numbers, etc., but no cases of specific superiority in these areas have been described, apart possibly from number. Even the case of Rajan, who provides the clearest evidence for a specific innate ability, presents problems of interpretation. His enhanced memory span was apparent for both numbers and letters, thus weakening any suggestion for a specific numerical system, but he did not show generally superior verbal ability, as would be expected if a single modular verbal-sequential system exists.

To conclude, the evidence examined does not encourage the conclusion that clear patterns of specific memory superiority exist which match subdivisions proposed on the basis of specific memory damage or psychometric evidence. It has already been pointed out that neuropsychological cases of specific memory loss indicate no more than that a necessary process for a particular memory task has been impaired. Cases of specific superiority in a task-specific component process of this kind are likely to be very rare and difficult to isolate. It has also been pointed out that the distinctions based on psychometric evidence are generally not defined sufficiently precisely to make clear predictions about possible patterns of memory superiority. It is, therefore, probably not surprising that no strong evidence has emerged for specific memory superiority that coheres well with the picture from these other methods of investigation.

A different type of specificity in memory expertise is, however, more clearly apparent in the cases of S, TM, and the autistic children (and possibly Subject H as well). In these cases there were limitations in processing material for its meaning and this led to a marked contrast in the ability of these subjects to retain physical and meaningful aspects of the input. In the case of S, this was apparently due to the vivid visual associations evoked by the input, associations that interfered with or prevented deeper analysis. (Conceivably one might ascribe these differences to higher efficiency of the PRS and lower efficiency of the integrative processes necessary for episodic memory.) To a lesser extent this was probably also true of TM and Subject H, but it is likely that their fixation with mnemonic methods, designed to encode arbitrary, meaningless material, had combined with a processing weakness and thus produced a marked difference in performance on meaningful and relatively meaningless material. The autistic children probably suffered from a similar weakness in semantic processing to an even greater degree. Hence, in these cases it is suggested that unusual encoding processes, possibly combined with restrictive strategies, were the causal antecedents of the contrasting memory abilities for arbitrary and meaningful material.

There is one more sense in which specificity of memory expertise has been indicated in the results discussed. Exceptional retention ability has been identified in the cases of Aitken, VP, ED, JR, and Subject J. In most of these cases (but not all) such ability was allied to superior memory performance after relatively short delays also. Immediate memory performance following limited exposure to the material, as tested in all the tasks employed in our studies, is presumed to be primarily an indication of encoding efficiency. However, neither ED nor Subject J scored highly on the immediate tasks, but both showed only about 5% loss over a week of the material retained in the immediate test, as did JR. These findings suggest that retention efficiency is separable from encoding efficiency, a conclusion reinforced by the results of the factor analysis described in Chapter 6. In fact, it is likely that superior retention is the single most significant characteristic of a naturally superior memory. A number of results discussed in Chapter 3 have already indicated the need to distinguish these different subprocesses of memory when considering overall performance (Ingham, 1952; Moss et al., 1986; Rabbitt, 1993b).

GENERAL FEATURES OF GOOD TECHNIQUES

These have already been discussed in detail at the end of Chapter 2. They require association of items to associates which already possess meaning (semanticisation), and linking of groups of such associations together into larger structures, either by creating associations or using existing pre-learned structures. These processes are facilitated by the use of imagery, but this is not essential. If the associations and structures are devised for or limited to encoding a specific type of material, superior performance will be restricted to that type of material, as in the case of Ericsson's subject SF. However, the principles underlying these methods are general ones and it is perfectly possible to apply them to a wide range of material, as TE and Subjects C and G in the memory champions sample demonstrated.

GENERAL NATURAL MEMORY ABILITY

Turning now to an examination of the evidence for superior general natural memory ability, the data from our studies described in Chapters 4 and 5 present a stronger case for a general natural ability than for superior operation of specific modular memory systems. Of the subjects described in Chapter 2, Aitken and VP demonstrated ability to recall a variety of material at a high level without use of specific strategies. S may or may not be another example of this ability, since it is unclear to what extent his strategies were the basis of his superior performance rather than a method of controlling the spontaneous operation of his memory system. Similarly TE depended heavily on strategies, yet excelled on a task which was not appropriate for them (story recall). The evidence for a general memory ability that is not based on strategies becomes much clearer in the case of some of the subjects described in Chapters 4 and 5. JR showed good performance over nearly all the tasks, and even if one of her best displays did depend on a simple strategy devised on the spot (word recall by linking the words in a story), her exceptional performance in name recall to pictures of faces, particularly after a week's delay, did not depend on any identifiable strategy. Together with the other good performers who claimed not to be using strategies (Subjects C and 36) she showed better performance on non-strategic than on strategic tasks, compared with the control group, and better performance than the strategic group on these non-strategic tasks. These subjects also demonstrated retention after a week that was well above that of the control group and the strategists.

Clearly it is not satisfactory to rely solely on self-report as the criterion for deciding whether or not a subject's performance is strategy-based. We have no reason to doubt that subjects report their own insights about the basis of their performance honestly, but it is possible that some depend on highly practised automatic processes, which once had to be learned but are no longer accessible to introspection. One problem with such an explanation is the absence of any plausible description of what such an effective all-purpose unconscious strategy might be. The strategy descriptions we do have all refer to deliberate, complex and often highly practised recoding devices which are either highly task specific or have to be consciously adapted in order to apply them to a variety of tasks. They are readily available to conscious awareness.

The main argument for accepting at face value subjects' own reports on their use or non-use of special methods was laid out in detail in Chapter 5, where some deductions of differences in performance, which might be predicted from differences in the use of strategies, were shown to be supported by the data. Findings strongly supporting the self-reported differences were that strategic subjects showed substantially worse performance on tasks where their methods were not readily applicable (compared both with non-strategists and their own performance on tasks amenable to strategies), whereas "naturals" showed a very similar level of performance on tasks unsuited to strategies and tasks suited to them. Non-strategists also performed better than strategists on non-strategic tasks. Furthermore, even though several qualifications were necessary about the delayed memory tests, the superiority of the natural group was striking and particularly the performance of JR.

Although we argue that we have firmly established the case for marked individual differences in natural general memory ability, there is almost no support in our data for ability of this nature, which is so unusual as to suggest some marked qualitative difference in brain organisation or function. It is difficult to specify precise criteria for the latter possibility. In general we would incline to such an explanation if performance were recorded that was so superior to that of the general population that no performance at an intermediate level between the normal and the superior is ever observed. JR's delayed recall of names to faces may meet this criterion.

The limiting case of performance meeting such a criterion would be ability to carry out a task that normals find completely impossible, even after practice. Some of the cases described by others and summarised in Chapter 2 may provide evidence for qualitative differences of this nature, such as Aitken's long-term retention and Stromeyer and Psotka's (1970) subject who could fuse random dot stereograms presented at a 24-hour interval. On the whole, such evidence is stronger for specific than for general memory abilities. In the latter case, the data we have gathered are suggestive rather of some individuals lying at the upper end of a normal distribution of memory ability, such that on most tasks they will outperform the general population substantially. Over all the tasks, if a compound measure is devised, they will lie at the very upper end of the distribution. The implication of such findings is that one or more processes, involved in all or most memorising, functions at a high level of efficiency in some individuals. There is a plethora of potential candidates at various levels of description. At the psychological level, possible candidates are depth or variety of coding, discrimination, efficiency of an integrative or binding process (see Chapter 3), inhibition of response competition, and retrieval efficiency. At a neural level, complexity or structure of connections might be responsible, while transmitter efficiency at a biochemical level is a further possibility (see Chapter 3).

These conclusions agree broadly with those drawn from correlational studies discussed in Chapter 3. It was pointed out there that the neuropsychological data have been assumed to support a modular system, while correlational studies suggest at least one broader general memory factor. It was further argued that neuropsychological results only indicate that a specific (and damaged) process is necessary to performance of a specific task, not that all processes required to perform that task are specific to it. Correlational studies, on the other hand, indicate that some processes are common to several tasks in the intact brain. The evidence from studies of superior memory supports this conclusion.

The analysis of data from all the subjects in our studies who did not admit to a systematic use of strategies (Chapter 6) offered further support for the existence of a general memory ability. There were high correlations between many of the tasks employed in the current studies (memory for names, word lists, telephone numbers, spatio-temporal positions of pictures, and snow crystals) and the Maximum Likelihood Factor analysis identified a strong factor on which all these tasks loaded, together with memory for a story and for faces and retention of words. This factor correlated highly and negatively with age. It has been suggested that it represents efficiency of initial encoding.

Further evidence emerged from this analysis supporting the findings in earlier correlational studies that memory for material recently experienced, as reflected in the Maximum Likelihood Factor analysis, may be at least partially distinct from ability to retain information over a longer period. Distinct factors for retention of the story and words and for retention of faces were also extracted. A possible reason for the differences between these two retention factors is the requirement for retrieval in story and word recall, but more evidence is needed on this point. The tasks we employed did not attempt to test retrieval systematically and future work needs to devise some method of doing this. This relatively clear picture is slightly confused by the loading of word retention on the first (encoding) factor, as well as the second (retention) factor.

CONCLUSIONS ON SPECIFIC AND GENERAL
MEMORY ABILITY

Summarising the evidence in relation to the first four main questions, subjects employing strategies can produce a very high level of performance, especially with less meaningful material such as numbers. This almost invariably seems to depend on recoding in order to make the material meaningful and reduce the load on memory. Such recoding requires either specially learned transformations or general knowledge, for example about properties of numbers.

Occasionally specific memory abilities occur that do not appear to depend on strategy. A variety of types have been reported but nearly all are isolated cases for which no further explanation is apparent. In some cases these abilities become overlaid with adopted strategies.

The generality of application of strategies varies with the strategy and the individual. Most are quite restricted in application, though some can be modified in order to apply them to different tasks. However, some tasks are not amenable to strategies due to their structure or novelty.

Strategies aid immediate memory and frequently also retention over longer intervals, for example by providing highly discriminable codes for otherwise meaningless material. However, in the study described in Chapter 5, the strategists did not generally retain material well over a week, compared with the naturals. There were a number of possible reasons for this, such as the practice of deliberate forgetting and interference by subsequent memory performances, so this important result needs further clarification. For example, are the strategists who have demonstrated good long-term recall, such as S and TE, just better strategists or did they possess natural memory ability as well?

Some subjects display good and even very good memory performance without describing any strategies. They perform as well on tasks not amenable to strategies (or better) than on tasks which are amenable, and they show superior retention without warning of a delayed test. We have categorised these as subjects with superior natural ability. Though the most striking cases show both excellent immediate recall and retention over a longer period, these two abilities are probably at least partly independent, as indicated by the performance of some subjects (ED and J) and the Maximum Likelihood Factor analysis reported in Chapter 6. It is suggested that the two abilities represent superior operation of encoding and retention processes respectively.

These conclusions imply that much (or all) memorising depends on some common processes, even though initial encoding may be done by different specific systems such as the PRS system discussed in Chapter 3. The common process could be an integrating or binding operation dependent on the hippocampal system, but at this stage this can only be speculation. This was discussed in detail in Chapter 3.

MEMORY ABILITY OF CLOSE RELATIVES AND EARLY AWARENESS OF SUPERIOR MEMORY ABILITY

Findings on the ability of near relatives and on early awareness of unusual memory ability were no more than suggestive and further data are needed before any conclusion can be drawn about these as possible criteria for classifying superior memory ability as natural.

RELATIONS BETWEEN AUTOBIOGRAPHICAL MEMORY AND MEMORY ABILITY IN LABORATORY TASKS

No evidence emerged that individuals with superior memory performance on our tasks also displayed above average ability to recall autobiographical detail from their past. However, the only measures of this were estimated age of recall of earliest memory and the amount of detail in that memory. There are considerable problems over the reliability and validity of the first measure especially, which is in most cases impossible to cross check with objective data. No differences were apparent between strategists and naturals or between the superior groups and the control group.

However, the analysis of the group data described in Chapter 6 did produce interesting evidence that detail in the earliest memory was related to aspects of memory measured by the laboratory tasks. More detailed earliest memories were associated with better overall performance on the memory tasks. Together with the results reported by Richardson (1994) on relations between imagery ability and access to early memories, there is considerable encouragement in these findings for pursuing this line of enquiry further.

MEMORY AND INTELLIGENCE

No compelling evidence has emerged for relations between aspects of memory measured in our studies and IQ, as measured by the Mill Hill vocabulary scale. The latter did correlate significantly with recall of the story, retention of faces, and (marginally) with detail in the earliest memory, but was not significantly related to any of the factors extracted by the Maximum Likelihood analysis, nor did strategic and natural memorisers differ on this measure. While many subjects in the Memoriad sample scored highly on the Mill Hill scale, some did not. High verbal IQ did seem to be associated with superior natural memory, while superior memory for meaningless material, combined with poor memory for meaningful material, was associated with Mill Hill scores in the average range in our sample, plus strong reliance on strategies. However, no general relation between Mill Hill scores and memory performance was apparent over the whole sample of subjects who did not employ strategies (see Chapter 6). These results are in general agreement with the conclusions from the literature discussed in Chapter 3, where it was argued that, while measures of Working Memory may be related to IQ measures, no strong evidence has emerged for any relation between long-term memory performance and measures of intelligence.

MEMORY AND IMAGERY

The IDQ and VVIQ were given only to TE (IDQ only), JR, TM, and the expert sample described in Chapter 5, so no comparisons with the control group or correlations could be carried out. All these 13 subjects scored significantly above the test norms for the imaginal component of the IDQ and many of them did the same on the verbal component (the exceptions were TE, JR, B, C, I, and J). On the VVIQ two subjects produced the maximum score, but even this is not significantly different from the mean of the norms we employed, so the measure is insensitive. The only significant relation between these measures and any of the memory scores was between verbal thinking on the IDQ and memory for Prime Ministers ($r = 0.67$, $P = 0.02$). Though this makes some sense it may well be a chance finding among the 36 correlations tested. Hence, the only conclusion that seems to emerge is that many experts in memory report that they are high in imaginal thinking and many of them report the same for verbal thinking. It is impossible to establish any causal relationships.

Several aspects of the matrix-learning task were designed to test the possibility of visual imagery. There was, however, no evidence that any subject was able to retain an eidetic image of the matrix. Subject B described a form of memory image, which he could develop over time in long-term memory, and Subject E alluded to a similar ability, but this was clearly an entirely different type of image from that employed by eidetickers. Subjects who learned the matrix by strategic methods and those who learned by rote showed similar patterns in recall times for specified rows and columns, suggesting that the final forms of their memories were similar.

FINAL THOUGHTS

At the beginning of this book we suggested that much could be learned about memory by studying superior performance, as well as impairments. We hope that we have demonstrated that the understanding of memory structure and processes can benefit greatly through an in-depth examination of unusually able individuals. With a few notable exceptions, this approach has been neglected. Though we have often been critical of the ideas of Anders Ericsson, we acknowledge the fruitfulness of the ideas he has derived from such an approach and the stimulus his work has often provided for our own ideas.

As so often, the work we have described raises more questions than it answers, but we hope some of them are important questions. We hope that we have highlighted the importance of studying individual differences in memory ability that are not dependent on special methods. The latter topic has been brilliantly investigated by Ericsson and his colleagues and placed in the wider context of the development of expertise in general. Since memory underlies virtually all cognitive performance, the topic of variation in natural memory ability deserves more attention than it has received to date. We hope that our work will stimulate such attention, by outlining some of the issues which need to be addressed, such as specificity versus generality, separability of component processes, heritability, and the place of memory in more general models of cognitive processes.

Some lines of investigation which might prove profitable are as follows. Further analysis of the processes used by mnemonic experts, for example by examining the impact of different types of interference, would help to delineate the nature, role, and characteristics of Working Memory, which underlies the encoding and retrieval processes on which expertise depends. Distinctions between superiority in encoding, retention, and retrieval clearly demand further analysis, as does the finding in the present studies that experts reliant on strategies did not show exceptional retention when they did not expect a delayed test. The memory abilities of close relatives of subjects demonstrating unusual natural memory ability would also repay investigation. Though it is almost impossible for the psychologist unambiguously to separate strategic and natural factors in memory performance, with the increasing sophistication of direct methods of recording brain activity, rapid advances are likely in methods of studying memory in action. Once these methods are available, we need to be clear about the questions that require an answer and we believe that the study of individuals with unusual ability helps to crystallise those questions and is likely to be crucial in seeking answers.

REFERENCES

Achard, G. (1989). *Rhétorique à Herennius*. Paris: Belles Lettres.

Allard, F., & Starkes, J.L. (1991). Motor-skill experts in sports, dance, and other domains. In K.A. Ericsson & J. Smith (Eds.), *Toward a general theory of expertise: Prospects and limits* (pp. 126–152). Cambridge, UK: Cambridge University Press.

Allison, R.B. (1960). *Learning parameters and human abilities* (Tech. Rep. No. 1). Princeton, NJ: Educational Testing Service and Princeton University.

Anderson, J.R. (1983). *The architecture of cognition*. Harvard, MA: Harvard University Press.

Anderson, M. (1992). *Intelligence and development*. Oxford, UK: Blackwell.

Anderson, R.E. (1976). Short-term retention of the where and when of pictures and words. *Journal of Experimental Psychology: General, 105*, 378–402.

Aristotle (1957). *Parva naturalia* (with English trans. by W.S. Hett). London: Heinemann.

Baddeley, A.D. (1986). *Working memory*. New York: Oxford University Press.

Baddeley, A.D. (1990). *Human memory: Theory and practice*. Hove, UK: Lawrence Erlbaum Associates Ltd.

Baddeley, A.D., & Hitch, G.J. (1974). Working memory. In G. Bower (Ed.), *The psychology of learning and motivation, Vol. 8* (pp. 47–90). New York: Academic Press.

Barlow, F. (1951). *Mental prodigies*. London: Hutchinson.

Baron-Cohen, S., Harrison, J., Goldstein, L.H., & Wyke, M. (1993). Coloured speech perception: Is synaesthesia what happens when modularity breaks down? *Perception, 22*, 419–426.

Baron-Cohen, S., Leslie, A.M., & Frith, U. (1985). Does the autistic child have a "theory of mind"? *Cognition, 21*, 31–46.

Baron-Cohen, S., Wyke, M.A., & Binnie, C. (1987). Hearing words and seeing colours: An experimental investigation of a case of synaesthesia. *Perception, 16*, 761–767.

Bartlett, F.C. (1932). *Remembering*. Cambridge, UK: Cambridge University Press.

Bennett, H.L. (1983). Remembering drink orders: The memory skills of cocktail waitresses. *Human Learning, 2*, 157–169.

Beyn, E.S., & Knyazeva, G.R. (1962). The problem of prosopagnosia. *Journal of Neurology, Neurosurgery and Psychiatry, 25*, 154–158.

Biederman, I., Cooper, E.E., Mahadevan, R.S., & Fox, P.W. (1992). Unexceptional spatial memory in an exceptional memorist. *Journal of Experimental Psychology: Learning, Memory and Cognition, 18*, 654–657.

Binet, A. (1894). *Psychologie des grands calculateurs et joueurs d'échecs*. Paris: Libraire Hachette.

Blaxton, T. (1989). Investigating dissociations among memory measures: Support for a transfer appropriate processing framework. *Journal of Experimental Psychology: Learning, Memory and Cognition, 15*, 657–668.

Blaxton, T.A. (1992). Dissociations among memory measures in memory-impaired subjects: Evidence for a processing account of memory. *Memory and Cognition, 20*, 549–562.

Bogyo, L., & Ellis, R. (1988). Elly: A study in contrasts. In L.K. Obler & D. Fein (Eds.), *The exceptional brain: The neuropsychology of talent and special abilities* (pp. 265–276). New York: The Guilford Press.

Bousfield, W.A., & Barry, H. (1933). The unusual memory of a lightning calculator. *American Journal of Psychology, 45*, 353–358.

Brown, E., & Deffenbacher, K. (1988). Superior memory performance and mnemonic encoding. In L.K. Obler & D. Fein (Eds.), *The exceptional brain: The neuropsychology of talent and special abilities* (pp. 191–211). New York: The Guilford Press.

Bryant, K.L. (1989). *The right hemisphere language battery*. Kibworth, UK: Far Communications.

Butters, N. (1989). *Dissociation of implicit memory in dementia*. Paper presented at the Meeting of the Psychonomic Society, Atlanta, Georgia.

Cabeza, R., & Ohta, N. (1993). Dissociating conceptual priming, perceptual priming and explicit memory. *European Journal of Cognitive Psychology, 5*, 35–54.

Cantor, J., Engle, R.W., & Hamilton, G. (1991). Short-term memory, working memory and verbal abilities: How do they relate? *Intelligence, 15*, 229–246.

Carpenter, P.A., Just, M.A., & Shell, P. (1990). What one intelligence test measures: A theoretical account of the processing in the Raven Progressive Matrices test. *Psychological Review, 97*, 404–431.

Carroll, J.B. (1993). *Human cognitive abilities: A survey of factor analytic studies*. Cambridge, UK: Cambridge University Press.

Ceci, S.J., deSimone, M., & Johnson, S. (1992). Memory in context: A case study of "Bubbles P", a gifted but uneven memoriser. In D.J. Herrmann, H. Weingartner, A. Searleman, & C. McEvoy (Eds.), *Memory improvement: Implications for memory theory* (pp. 169–186). New York: Springer-Verlag.

Ceci, S.J., & Liker, J.K. (1986). A day at the races: A study of IQ, expertise and cognitive complexity. *Journal of Experimental Psychology: General, 115*, 255–266.

Chaffin, R., & Imreh, G. (1994, August). *Memorizing for piano performance*. Unpublished paper presented at Third Practical Aspects of Memory Conference, Washington.

Charness, N. (1988). Expertise in chess, music and physics: A cognitive perspective. In L.K. Obler & D. Fein (Eds.), *The exceptional brain: The neuropsychology of talent and special abilities* (pp. 399–426). New York: The Guilford Press.

Chase, W.G., & Ericsson, K.A. (1981). Skilled memory. In J.R. Anderson (Ed.), *Cognitive skills and their acquisition* (pp. 141–189). London: Lawrence Erlbaum Associates Ltd.

Chase, W.G., & Ericsson, K.A. (1982). Skill and working memory. In G.H. Bower (Ed.), *The psychology of learning and motivation, Vol. 16* (pp. 1–58). New York: Academic Press.

Cicero, M.T. (1942). *De oratore* (with English trans. by H. Rackham). London: Heinemann.

Cohen, R.L., & Sandberg, T. (1977). Relations between intelligence and short-term memory. *Cognitive Psychology, 9*, 534–554.

Coltheart, M., & Glick, M.J. (1974). Visual imagery: A case study. *Quarterly Journal of Experimental Psychology, 26*, 438–453.

Cowan, N., Braine, M.D.S., & Leavitt, L.A. (1985). The phonological and metaphonological representation of speech: Evidence from fluent backward talkers. *Journal of Memory and Language, 24*, 679–698.

Cowan, N., & Leavitt, L.A. (1982). Talking backward: Exceptional speech play in late childhood. *Journal of Child Language, 9*, 481–495.

Cowan, N., & Leavitt, L.A. (1987). The developmental course of two children who could talk backward five years ago. *Journal of Child Language, 14*, 393–395.

Cowan, N., Leavitt, L.A., Massaro, D.W., & Kent, R.D. (1982). A fluent backward talker. *Journal of Speech and Hearing Research, 25*, 48–53.

Craik, F.I.M., & Lockhart, R.S. (1972). Levels of processing: A framework for memory research. *Journal of Verbal Learning and Verbal Behaviour, 11*, 671–684.

Crowder, R.G. (1993). Systems and principles in memory theory: Another critique of pure memory. In A.F. Collins, S.E. Gathercole, M.A. Conway, & P.E. Morris (Eds.), *Theories of memory* (pp. 139–161). Hove, UK: Lawrence Erlbaum Associates Ltd.

Cytowic, R.E. (1989). *Synaesthesia: A union of the senses*. Berlin, Germany: Springer.

Cytowic, R.E., & Wood, F.B. (1982). Synaesthesia: A review of major theories and their brain bases. *Brain and Cognition, 1*, 23–35.

Daneman, M., & Carpenter, P.A. (1980). Individual differences in working memory and reading. *Journal of Verbal Learning and Verbal Behaviour, 19*, 450–466.

Daniel, A. (1981). *The effects of vividness of mental imagery and relaxation level on recall of childhood memories.* Unpublished honours thesis, Department of Psychology, University of Western Australia.

Datas (1904). *Memory by Datas: A simple system of memory training.* London: Gale & Poulden.

Davidoff, J., & Wilson, B. (1985). A case of visual agnosia showing a disorder of pre-semantic vision classification. *Cortex, 21,* 121–134.

Dempster, F. (1985). Proactive interference in sentence recall: Topic similarity effects and individual differences. *Memory and Cognition, 13,* 81–89.

Denis, M. (1987). Individual imagery differences and prose processing. In M.A. McDaniel & M. Pressley (Eds.), *Imagery and related mneumonic processes: Theories, individual differences, and applications.* New York: Springer-Verlag.

Denis, M., Engelkamp, J., & Mohr, G. (1991) Memory of imagined actions: Imagining yourself or another person. *Psychological Research, 53,* 246–250.

De Renzi, E., Liotti, M., & Nichelli, N. (1987). Semantic amnesia with preservation of auto-biographic memory: A case study. *Cortex, 23,* 575–597.

Dube, F. (1977). *A cross-cultural study of the relationship between 'intelligence' level and story recall.* Doctoral dissertation, Cornell University. (Abridged version in U. Neisser (Ed.) (1982), *Memory observed.* San Francisco: Freeman.)

Ellis, N.C., & Hennelly, R.A. (1980). A bilingual word-length effect: Implications for intelligence testing and the relative ease of mental calculation in Welsh and English. *British Journal of Psychology, 71,* 43–51.

Ericsson, K.A. (1985). Memory skill. *Canadian Journal of Psychology, 39,* 188 231.

Ericsson, K.A. (1988). Analysis of memory performance in terms of skill. In R.J. Sternberg (Ed.), *Advances in the psychology of human intelligence, Vol. 4* (pp. 137–179). Hillsdale, NJ: Lawrence Erlbaum Associates Inc.

Ericsson, K.A., & Chase, W.G. (1982). Exceptional memory. *American Scientist, 70,* 607–615.

Ericsson, K.A., Chase, W.G., & Falloon, S. (1980). Acquisition of memory skill. *Science, 208,* 1181–1182.

Ericsson, K.A., & Faivre, I.A. (1988). What's exceptional about exceptional abilities? In L.K. Obler & D. Fein (Eds.), *The exceptional brain: The neuropsychology of talent and special abilities* (pp. 436–473). New York: The Guilford Press.

Ericsson, K.A., & Polson, P.G. (1988a). A cognitive analysis of exceptional memory for restaurant orders. In M. Chi, R. Glaser, & M. Farr (Eds.), *The nature of expertise* (pp. 23–70). Hillsdale, NJ: Lawrence Erlbaum Associates Inc.

Ericsson, K.A., & Polson, P.G. (1988b). An experimental analysis of the mechanisms of a memory skill. *Journal of Experimental Psychology: Learning, Memory and Cognition, 14,* 305–316.

Ericsson, K.A., & Simon, H. (1980). Verbal reports as data. *Psychological Review, 87,* 215–251.

Ericsson, K.A., & Simon, H.A. (1984). *Protocol analysis.* Cambridge, MA: MIT Press.

Ernest, C.H. (1977). Imagery ability and cognition: A critical review. *Journal of Mental Imagery, 2,* 181–216.

Finkel, D., Pedersen, N., & McGue, M. (1993). Genetic influences on memory performance in adulthood: Comparison of Minnesota and Swedish twin data. *Psychology and Aging, 10,* 437–446.

Goldstein, A.G., & Chance, J.E. (1970). Visual recognition memory for complex configurations. *Perception and Psychophysics, 9,* 237–241.

Gordon, P., Valentine, E., & Wilding, J. (1984). One man's memory: A study of a mnemonist. *British Journal of Psychology, 75,* 1–14.

Grafman, J., & Weingartner, H. (1995). A combinatorial binding and strength (CBS) model of memory: Is it a better framework for amnesia? In D. Herrmann, M. Johnson, C. McEvoy, C. Hertzog, & P. Hertel (Eds.), *Basic and applied memory research: Theory in context, Vol. I* (pp. 259–276). Hove, UK: Lawrence Erlbaum Associates Ltd.

Grierson, M. (1952). *Donald Francis Tovey: A biography based on letters.* London: Oxford University Press.

Gummerman, K., & Gray, C.R. (1971). Recall of visually presented material: An unwonted case and a bibliography for eidetic imagery. *Psychonomic Monograph Supplements, 4* (10), (Whole No. 58), 189–195.

Hancock, J. (1995). *Jonathan Hancock's mindpower system.* London: Hodder & Stoughton.

Hancock, J. (1996). *Mega memory.* London: Hodder Children's Books.

Hanggi, D. (1989). Differential aspects of visual short- and long-term memory. *European Journal of Cognitive Psychology, 1,* 285–292.

Hanley, J.R., Pearson, N.A., & Young, A.W. (1990). Impaired memory for new visual forms. *Brain, 113,* 1131–1148.

Hanley, J.R., & Young, A.W. (1994). The cognitive psychology of memory. In P.E. Morris & M. Gruneberg (Eds.), *Theoretical aspects of memory* (2nd edn; pp. 238–272). London: Routledge.

Hasher, L., & Zacks, R.T. (1979). Automatic and effortful processes in memory. *Journal of Experimental Psychology: General, 108,* 356–388.

Haywood, M.C., & Heal, L.H. (1968). Retention of learned visual associations as a function of IQ and learning levels. *American Journal of Mental Deficiency, 72,* 828–838.

Hegge, T. (1929). Some incidental memory experiments with the memory prodigy, Dr. Rückle. *Michigan Academy of Sciences, Arts and Letters, 10,* 389–396.

Heindel, W.C., Butters, N., & Salmon, D.P. (1988). Impaired learning of a motor skill in patients with Huntington's disease. *Behavioural Neuroscience, 102,* 141–147.

Hishitani, S. (1985). Imagery differences and task characteristics in memory. In D.F. Marks & D.G. Russell (Eds.), *Imagery 1: Proceedings of the first international imagery conference* (pp. 5–13). Dunedin, New Zealand: Human Performance Associates.

Hoosain, R., & Salili, F. (1987). Language differences in pronunciation speed for numbers, digit span and mathematical ability. *Psychologia, 30,* 34–38.

Hunt, E. (1980). Intelligence as an information-processing concept. *British Journal of Psychology, 71,* 449–474.

Hunt, E., & Love, T. (1972). How good can memory be? In A.W. Melton & E. Martin (Eds.), *Coding processes in human memory* (pp. 237–250). New York: Wiley.

Hunt, E., Lunneborg, C., & Lewis, J. (1975). What does it mean to be high verbal? *Cognitive Psychology, 7,* 194–227.

Hunter, I.M.L. (1962). An exceptional talent for calculative thinking. *British Journal of Psychology, 53,* 243–258.

Hunter, I.M.L. (1977). An exceptional memory. *British Journal of Psychology, 68,* 155–164.

Hunter, I.M.L. (1990). Exceptional memory performers. In M.J.A. Howe (Ed.), *Encouraging the development of exceptional skills and talents.* Leicester, UK: BPS Books.

Hunter, I.M.L. (1996). *Remembering a story after 26 years.* Unpublished paper.

Ingham, J.G. (1952). Memory and intelligence. *British Journal of Psychology, 43,* 20–32.

Intons-Peterson, M.J., & Smyth, M.M. (1987). The anatomy of repertory memory. *Journal of Experimental Psychology: Learning, Memory and Cognition, 13,* 490–500.

Isaac, A.R., & Marks, D.F. (1994). Individual differences in mental imagery experience: Developmental changes and specialisation. *British Journal of Psychology, 85,* 479–500.

Jensen, A.R., & Figueroa, R.A. (1975). Forward and backward digit-span interaction with race and IQ: Predictions from Jensen's theory. *Journal of Educational Psychology, 67,* 882–893.

Jones, H.E. (1926). Phenomenal memorising as a "special ability". *Journal of Applied Psychology, 10*, 367–377.

Judd, T. (1988). The varieties of musical talent. In L.K. Obler & D. Fein (Eds.), *The exceptional brain: The neuropsychology of talent and special abilities* (pp. 127–155). New York: The Guilford Press.

Jurden, F.H. (1995). Individual differences in working memory and complex cognition. *Journal of Educational Psychology, 87*, 93–102.

Kanner, L. (1943). Autistic disturbances of affective contact. *Nervous Child, 2*, 217–250.

Kapur, N., Heath, P., Meudell, P., & Kennedy, P. (1986). Amnesia can facilitate performance: Evidence from a patient with dissociated retrograde amnesia. *Neuropsychologia, 24*, 215–222.

Keane, M.M., Gabrieli, J.D.E., Fennema, A.C., Gordon, J.H., & Corkin, S. (1991). Evidence for a dissociation between perceptual and conceptual priming in Alzheimer's disease. *Behavioural Neuroscience, 105*, 326–342.

Klausmeier, H.J., & Feldhusen, J.F. (1959). Retention of arithmetic among children of low, average and high intelligence at 117 months of age. *Journal of Educational Psychology, 50*, 88–92.

Kliegl, R., Smith, J., Heckhausen, J., & Baltes, P.B. (1987). Mnemonic training for the acquisition of skilled digit memory. *Cognition and Instruction, 4*, 203–223.

Kyllonen, P., & Christal, R. (1990). Reasoning ability is (little more than) working-memory capacity?! *Intelligence, 14*, 389–433.

Landis, T., Cummings, J.L., Benson, D.F., & Palmer, E.P. (1986). Loss of topographical familiarity: An environmental agnosia. *Archives of Neurology, 43*, 132–136.

Lashley, K.S. (1929). *Brain mechanisms and intelligence: A quantitative study of injuries of the brain.* Chicago: Chicago University Press.

Levine, D.N., Warach, J., & Farah, M. (1985). Two visual systems in mental imagery: Dissociation of what and where in imagery disorders due to bilateral posterior cerebral lesions. *Neurology, 35*, 1010–1018.

Lindenberger, U., Kliegl, R., & Baltes, P.B. (1992). Professional expertise does not eliminate age differences in imagery-based memory performance during adulthood. *Psychology and Aging, 7*, 585–593.

Lorayne, H. (1958). *How to develop a super-power memory.* Preston, UK: Thomas.

Lord, A.B. (1960). *The singer of tales.* Cambridge, MA: Harvard University Press. (Excerpted in U. Neisser (Ed.) (1982), *Memory observed* (pp. 243–257)). San Francisco: Freeman.

Lucci, D., Fein, D., Holevas, A., & Kaplan, E. (1988). Paul: A musically gifted autistic boy. In L.K. Obler & D. Fein (Eds.), *The exceptional brain: The neuropsychology of talent and special abilities* (pp. 310–324). New York: The Guilford Press.

Luria, A.R. (1975). *The mind of a mnemonist.* Harmondsworth, UK: Penguin.

Mackintosh, N. (1986). The biology of intelligence? *British Journal of Psychology, 77*, 1–18.

MacLeod, C.M., Hunt, E.B., & Mathews, N.N. (1978). Individual differences in the verification of sentence–picture relationships. *Journal of Verbal Learning and Verbal Behaviour, 17*, 493–507.

Manturzewska, M. (1960). *Psychologiczne Warunki Osiagniec Pianistycznych* [Psychological conditions and piano playing]. Wroclaw, Poland: Ossolineum.

Marks, D.F. (1973). Visual memory differences in the recall of pictures. *British Journal of Psychology, 64*, 17–24.

Marschark, M., & Surian, L. (1989). Why does imagery aid memory? *European Journal of Cognitive Psychology, 1*, 251–263.

McGeorge, P., Crawford, J.R., & Kelly, S.W. (in press). The relationship between psychometric intelligence and learning in an explicit and an implicit task. *Journal of Experimental Psychology: Learning, Memory and Cognition.*

McKelvie, S.J. (1978). Sex differences in facial memory. In M.M. Gruneberg, P.E. Morris, & R.N. Sykes (Eds.), *Practical aspects of memory*. London: Academic Press.

McKelvie, S.J. (1995). The VVIQ as a psychometric test of individual differences in visual imagery vividness: A critical quantitative review and plea for direction. *Journal of Mental Imagery, 19*, 1–106.

Miklaszewski, K. (1989). A case study of a pianist preparing a musical performance. *Psychology of Music, 17*, 95–109.

Miller, L.K. (1989). *Musical savants: Exceptional skill in the mentally retarded*. Hove, UK: Lawrence Erlbaum Associates Ltd.

Miller, L.T., & Vernon, P.A. (1992). The general factor in short-term memory, intelligence, and reaction time. *Intelligence, 16*, 5–29.

Mishkin, M., & Appenzeller, T. (1987). The anatomy of memory. *Scientific American, 256*, 80–89.

Mohindra, N.K. (1983). *Noise effects on rate of rehearsal in short term memory*. Unpublished PhD thesis, University of London.

Morris, P.E., Jones, S., & Hampson, P. (1978). An imagery mnemonic for the learning of people's names. *British Journal of Psychology, 69*, 335–336.

Morton, J.A. (1970). A functional model for memory. In D.A. Norman (Ed.), *Models of human memory*. New York: Academic Press.

Moss, M.B., Albert, M.S., Butters, N., & Payne, M. (1986). Differential patterns of memory loss among patients with Alzheimer's disease, Huntington's disease and Alcoholic Korsakoff's syndrome. *Archives of Neurology, 43*, 239–246.

Mukunda, K.V., & Hall, V.C. (1992). Does performance on memory for order correlate with performance on standardized measures of ability? A meta-analysis. *Intelligence, 16*, 81–97.

Müller, G. (1911). Sur Analyse der Gedächtnistätigkeit und des Vorstellungs verlaufes. *Zeitschrift für Psychologie, Erganzungsband, 5*, 7–367.

Müller, G. (1913). Neue versuche mit Rückle. *Zeitschrift für Psychologie, 7*, 193–213.

Nadel, L. (1994). Multiple memory systems: What and why? An update. In D.L. Schacter & E. Tulving (Eds.), *Memory systems 1994* (pp. 39–63). Cambridge, MA: MIT Press.

Nelson, K. (1993). Explaining the emergence of autobiographical memory. In A.F. Collins, S.E. Gathercole, M.A. Conway, & P.E. Morris (Eds.), *Theories of memory* (pp. 355–385). Hove, UK: Lawrence Erlbaum Associates Ltd.

Neisser, U. (1982). *Memory observed*. San Francisco: Freeman.

Nettelbeck, T., & Rabbitt, P.M.A. (1992). Aging, cognitive performance and mental speed. *Intelligence, 16*, 189–205.

Newell, A. (1990). *Unified theories of cognition*. Cambridge, MA: Harvard University Press.

Noice, H. (1991). The role of explanation and plan recognition in the learning of theatrical scripts. *Cognitive Science, 15*, 425–460.

Noice, H. (1992). Elaborative memory strategies of professional actors. *Applied Cognitive Psychology, 6*, 417–427.

Noice, H. (1993). Effects of rote versus gist strategy on the verbatim retention of theatrical scripts. *Applied Cognitive Psychology, 7*, 75–84.

Noice, H., & Noice, T. (1993). The effects of segmentation on the recall of theatrical material. *Poetics, 22*, 51–67.

Noice, H., & Noice, T. (1996). Two approaches to learning a theatrical script. *Memory, 4*, 1–18.

Novoa, L., Fein, D., & Obler, L.K. (1988). Talent in foreign languages: A case study. In L.K. Obler & D. Fein (Eds.), *The exceptional brain: The neuropsychology of talent and special abilities* (pp. 294–302). New York: The Guilford Press.

Obler, L.K., & Fein, D. (1988). *The exceptional brain: The neuropsychology of talent and special abilities.* New York: The Guilford Press.

O'Brien, D. (1993). *How to develop a perfect memory.* London: Pavilion Books.

O'Keefe, J., & Nadel, L. (1978). *The hippocampus as a cognitive map.* Oxford, UK: Oxford University Press.

Oliver, W.L., & Ericsson, K.A. (1986). *Repertory actors' memory for their parts.* Paper presented at Eighth Annual conference of the Cognitive Science Society, Amherst, Massachusetts.

Osborn, H.F. (1902). Rapid memorizing: "Winging a part", as a lost faculty. *Psychological Review, 9,* 183–184.

Ostergard, A.L. (1994). Dissociations between word priming effects in normal subjects and patients with memory disorders: Multiple memory systems or retrieval? *Quarterly Journal of Experimental Psychology, 47a,* 331–364.

Paivio, A. (1971). *Imagery and verbal processes.* New York: Holt, Rinehart & Winston.

Paivio, A., & Harshman, R. (1983). Factor analysis of a questionnaire on imagery and verbal habits and skills. *Canadian Journal of Psychology, 37,* 461–483.

Pallis, C.A. (1955). Impaired identification of faces and places with agnosia for colours. *Journal of Neurology, Neurosurgery and Psychiatry, 18,* 218–224.

Park, C.C. (1967). *The siege: The first eight years of an autistic child.* New York: Harcourt, Brace & World.

Perruchet, P., & Baveux, P. (1989). Correlational analyses of explicit and implicit memory performance. *Memory and Cognition, 17,* 77–86.

Plomin, R. (1988). The nature and nurture of cognitive abilities. In R.J. Sternberg (Ed.), *Advances in the psychology of human intelligence, Vol. 4* (pp. 1–33). Hillsdale, NJ: Lawrence Erlbaum Associates Ltd.

Powers, P.A., Andriks, J.L., & Loftus, E.F. (1979). Eyewitness accounts of females and males. *Journal of Applied Psychology, 64,* 339–347.

Quintilian (1921–1922). *Institutio oratoria* (with English trans. by H.E. Butler). London: Heinemann.

Rabbitt, P.M.A. (1993a). Crystal quest: A search for the basis of maintenance of practised skills into old age. In A. Baddeley & L. Weiskrantz (Eds.), *Attention: Selection, awareness and control; A tribute to Donald Broadbent* (pp. 188–230). Oxford, UK: Clarendon Press.

Rabbitt, P. (1993b). Does it all go together when it goes? The Nineteenth Bartlett Memorial Lecture. *Quarterly Journal of Experimental Psychology, 46a,* 385–434.

Ratcliff, G., & Newcombe, F. (1982). Object recognition: Some deductions from clinical evidence. In A.W. Ellis (Ed.), *Normality and pathology in cognitive function.* London: Academic Press.

Reber, A.S. (1992). The cognitive unconscious: An evolutionary perspective. *Consciousness and Cognition, 1,* 93–133.

Reber, A.S., Walkenfeld, F.F., & Hernstadt, R. (1991). Implicit and explicit learning: Individual differences and IQ. *Journal of Experimental Psychology: Learning, Memory and Cognition, 17,* 888–896.

Reichard, G.A., Jakobson, R., & Werth, E. (1949). Language and synaesthesia. *Word, 5,* 224–233.

Restle, F. (1974). Critique of pure memory. In R.L. Solso (Ed.), *Theories in cognitive psychology: The Loyola symposium* (pp. 203–217). Hillsdale, NJ: Lawrence Erlbaum Associates Inc.

Richardson, A. (1994). *Individual differences in imaging: Their measurement, origins and consequences.* New York: Baywood.

Richardson, J.T.E., Cermak, L.S., Blackford, S.P., & O'Connor, M. (1987). The efficacy of imagery mnemonics following brain damage. In M.A. McDaniel & M. Pressley (Eds.),

Imagery and related mnemonic processes: Theories, individual differences and applications (pp. 303–328). New York: Springer-Verlag.

Riddoch, M.J., & Humphreys, G.W. (1987). *To see but not to see: A case study of visual agnosia.* London: Lawrence Erlbaum Associates Ltd.

Rimland, B. (1964). *Infantile autism: The syndrome and its implications for a neural theory of behaviour.* New York: Appleton-Century-Crofts.

Rohwer, W.D., Jr. (1970). Images and pictures in children's learning: Research results and instructional implications. In H.W. Reese (Chmn.), Imagery in children's learning: A symposium. *Psychological Bulletin, 73,* 393–403.

Rose, S.P.R. (1993). *The making of memory.* London: Bantam Books.

Rozin, P. (1976). The evolution of intelligence and access to the cognitive unconscious. *Progress in Psychobiology and Physiological Psychology, 6,* 245–280.

Rubin, D.C. (1995). *Memory in oral traditions.* New York: Oxford University Press.

Rule, W.R., & Jarrell, G.R. (1983). Intelligence and earliest memory. *Perceptual and Motor Skills, 56,* 795–798.

Sadoski, M., & Quast, Z. (1990). Reader response and long-term recall for journalistic text: The roles of imagery, affect, and importance. *Reading Research Quarterly, 25,* 256–272.

Saint-Cyr, J.A., Taylor, A.E., & Lang, A.E. (1988). Procedural learning and neostriatal dysfunction in man. *Brain, 111,* 941–959.

Salthouse, T.A. (1985). *A theory of cognitive aging.* Amsterdam: North Holland.

Sandor, B. (1932). The functioning of memory and the methods of mathematical prodigies. *Character and Personality, 1,* 70–74.

Schacter, D.L. (1992). Understanding implicit memory: A cognitive neuroscience approach. In A.F. Collins, S.E. Gathercole, M.A. Conway, & P.E. Morris (Eds.), *Theories of Memory* (pp. 387–412). Hove, UK: Lawrence Erlbaum Associates Ltd.

Schacter, D.L., & Tulving, E. (1994). What are the memory systems of 1994? In D.L. Schacter & E. Tulving (Eds.), *Memory systems 1994* (pp. 1–38). Cambridge, MA: MIT Press.

Schweizer, K. (1993). Verbal ability and speed of information-processing. *Personality and Individual Differences, 15,* 645–652.

Sheehan, P.W., & Neisser, U. (1969). Some variables affecting the vividness of imagery in recall. *British Journal of Psychology, 60,* 71–80.

Shepard, R.N. (1967) Recognition memory for words, sentences and pictures. *Journal of Verbal Learning and Verbal Behavior, 6,* 156–163.

Sloboda, J.A., Hermelin, B., & O'Connor, N. (1985). An exceptional musical memory. *Musical Perception, 3,* 155–170.

Sperling, G. (1960). The information available in brief visual presentations. *Psychological Monographs, 74,* 1–29.

Squire, L.R., Knowlton, B., & Musen, G. (1993). The structure and organization of memory. *Annual Review of Psychology, 44,* 453–495.

Stake, R.E. (1961). Learning parameters, aptitudes and achievements. *Psychometric Monographs, 9.*

Standing, L., Conezio, J., & Haber, R.N. (1970). Perception and memory for pictures: Single trial learning of 2500 visual stimuli. *Psychonomic Science, 19,* 73–74.

Stigler, J., Lee, S.-Y., & Stevenson, H. (1986). Digit memory in Chinese and English: Evidence for a temporally limited store. *Cognition, 23,* 1–20.

Stratton, G. (1982). The mnemonic feat of the "Shass Pollak". Abridged version in U. Neisser (Ed.), *Memory observed.* San Francisco: Freeman. (Original work published 1917).

Stromeyer, C.F., & Psotka, J. (1970). The detailed texture of eidetic images. *Nature, 225,* 346–349.

Susukita, T. (1933). Untersuchung eines ausserordentlichen Gedächtnisses in Japan (I). *Tohoku Psychologica Folia, 1,* 111–134.

Susukita, T. (1934). Untersuchung eines ausserordentlichen Gedächtnisses in Japan (II). *Tohoku Psychologica Folia, 2*, 15–42.

Tanwar, U., & Malhotra, D. (1990). Imagery variables in short term memory. *Psychological Studies, 35*, 191–196.

Tanwar, U., & Malhotra, D. (1992a). Interactive effects of personality and imagery variables in short term memory. *Psychologia, 35*, 55–61.

Tanwar, U., & Malhotra, D. (1992b). Short-term memory as a function of personality and imagery. *Personality and Individual Differences, 13*, 175–180.

Thompson, C.P., Cowan, T., & Frieman, J. (1993). *Memory search by a memorist*. London: Lawrence Erlbaum Associates Ltd.

Thompson, C.P., Cowan, T., Frieman, J., Mahadevan, R.S., Vogl, R.J., & Frieman, J. (1991). Rajan: A study of a memorist. *Journal of Memory and Language, 30*, 702–724.

Thorndyke, P.W. (1977). Cognitive studies in comprehension and memory in narrative discourse. *Cognitive Psychology, 9*, 77–110.

Tresch, M.C., Sinnamon, H.M., & Seamon, J.G. (1993). Double dissociation of spatial and object visual memory: Evidence from selective interference in intact human subjects. *Neuropsychologia, 31*, 211–219.

Tulving, E., Hayman, C.A.G., & Macdonald, C.A. (1991). Long-lasting perceptual priming and semantic learning in amnesia: A case experiment. *Journal of Experimental Psychology: Learning, Memory and Cognition, 17*, 595–617.

Ungeleider, L.G., & Mishkin, M. (1982). Two cortical visual systems. In D.J. Ingle, M.A. Goodale, & R.J.W. Mansfield (Eds.), *Analysis of visual behaviour* (pp. 549–586). Cambridge, MA: MIT Press.

Warren, E., & Groom, D. (1984). Memory test performance under three different waveforms of ECT for depression. *British Journal of Psychiatry, 144*, 370–375.

Waterhouse, L. (1988). Speculations on the neuroanatomical substrate of special talents. In L.K. Obler & D. Fein (Eds.), *The exceptional brain: The neuropsychology of talent and special abilities* (pp. 493–512). New York: The Guilford Press.

Weinland, J.D. (1948). The memory of Salo Finkelstein. *Journal of General Psychology, 39*, 243–257.

Weiskrantz, L. (1982). Comparative aspects of studies of amnesia. *Philosophical Transactions of the Royal Society of London, B298*, 97–109.

Wicinski, A.A. (1950). Psichologiceskii analiz processa raboty pianista-ispolnitiela nad muzykalnym proizviedieniem [Psychological analysis of piano performer's process of work on musical composition]. *Izviestia Akademii Piedagogiceskich Nauk Vyprosi* (Moscow), 171–215.

Wilding, J., Rashid, W., Gilmore, D., & Valentine, E. (1986). A comparison of two mnemonic methods in learning medical information. *Human Learning, 5*, 211–217.

Wilding, J., & Valentine, E. (1985). One man's memory for prose, faces and names. *British Journal of Psychology, 76*, 215–219.

Wilding, J., & Valentine, E. (1988). Searching for superior memories. In M.M. Gruneberg, P.E. Morris, & R.N. Sykes (Eds.), *Practical aspects of memory: Current research and issues: Vol. I. Memory in everyday life* (pp. 472–477). Chichester, UK: Wiley.

Wilding, J., & Valentine, E. (1991). Superior memory ability. In J. Weinman & J. Hunter (Eds.), *Memory: Neurochemical and abnormal perspectives* (pp. 209–228). Chur, Switzerland: Harwood.

Wilding, J., & Valentine, E. (1994a). Memory champions. *British Journal of Psychology, 85*, 231–244.

Wilding, J., & Valentine, E. (1994b). Mnemonic wizardry with the telephone directory—but stories are another story. *British Journal of Psychology, 85*, 501–509.

Witherspoon, D., & Moscovitch, M. (1989). Stochastic independence between two implicit memory tasks. *Journal of Experimental Psychology: Learning, Memory and Cognition, 15,* 22–30.

Yates, F.A. (1966). *The art of memory.* Harmondsworth, UK: Penguin.

Zeki, S. (1992). The visual image in mind and brain. *Scientific American,* September, 43–50.

Zeki, S. (1993). *A vision of the brain.* Oxford, UK: Blackwell.

Appendix

Formula for estimating the standard error of a distribution of scores from a regression line with one predictor variable (e.g. age), in order to calculate the z score of a new single individual on the dependent variable:

$$s.e. = \left(meansquare_e \left(1 + \frac{1}{n} + \frac{x^2}{SS_x} \right) \right)^{\frac{1}{2}}$$

where:

meansquare$_e$ is the mean squared error of the dependent variable from the regression line;

n = number of subjects contributing to the regression equation;

x = deviation of the new single subject from the mean score of the group on the predictor variable.

With two predictor variables (e.g. age and Mill Hill vocabulary score and deviations x_1 and x_2) the equation is:

$$s.e. = meansquare_e \left(1 + \frac{1}{n} \sum_{}^{2} c_{ii} x_i^2 + 2c_{12} x_1 x_2 \right)$$

where

$$C_{11} = \frac{SS_2}{SS_1 SS_2 - SP_{12}^2}$$

$$C_{12} = \frac{-SP_{12}}{SS_1 SS_2 - SP_{12}^2}$$

$$C_{21} = \frac{-SP_{12}}{SS_1 SS_2 - SP_{12}^2}$$

$$C_{22} = \frac{SS_1}{SS_1 SS_2 - SP_{12}^2}$$

and SS$_1$ and SS$_2$ are the sums of squares of the first and second predictor

Author Index

Achard, G., 9
Albert, M.S., 66, 69, 154
Allard, F., 53
Allison, R.B., 78
Anderson, J.R., 76
Anderson, M., 76, 77, 78
Anderson, R.E., 91
Andriks, J.L., 76
Appenzeller, T., 65
Aristotle, 9

Baddeley, A.D., 61, 66
Baltes, P.B., 36, 82
Barlow, F., 10, 52
Baron-Cohen, S., 25, 27
Barry, H., 19
Bartlett, F.C., 30
Baveux, P., 63
Bennett, H.L., 36
Benson, D.F., 65
Beyn, E.S., 65
Biederman, I., 37, 39, 65
Binet, A., 11
Binnie, C., 25
Blackford, S.P., 80
Blaxton, T., 63
Bogyo, L., 49
Bousfield, W.A., 19
Braine, M.D.S., 48
Brown, E., 11
Bryant, K.L., 111
Butters, N., 63, 66, 69, 154

Cabeza, R., 63
Cantor, J., 75
Carpenter, P.A., 74
Carroll, J.B., 68, 73, 77
Ceci, S.J., 21, 42, 43, 44, 76, 78
Cermak, L.S., 80
Chaffin, R., 51
Chance, J.E., 91
Charness, N., 22, 33, 34, 35, 58
Chase, W.G., 22, 33, 34, 35, 58
Christal, R., 74
Cicero, M.T., 9
Cohen, R.L., 75
Coltheart, M., 21, 48, 114, 153
Conezio, J., 5
Cooper, E.E., 21, 37, 38 39, 65
Corkin, S., 63
Cowan, N., 48
Cowan, T., 21, 37, 38
Craik, F.I.M., 69
Crawford, J.R., 78
Crowder, R.G., 69
Cummings, J.L., 65
Cytowic, R.E., 26

Daneman, M., 74
Daniel, A., 82
Davidoff, J., 10
De Renzi, E., 65
Deffenbacher, K., 11
Dempster, F., 75
Denis, M., 80, 81

DeSimone, M., 21, 42, 43, 44
Dube, F., 32, 78

Ellis, N.C., 45
Ellis, R., 49
Engelkamp, J., 80
Engle, R.W., 75
Ericsson, K.A., 11, 21, 22, 33, 34, 35, 36, 48, 52, 56, 57, 58, 73
Ernest, C.H., 81

Faivre, I.A., 33, 48, 56, 73
Falloon, S., 33
Farah, M., 65
Fein, D., 21, 22, 47, 49, 51, 152
Feldhusen, J.F., 78
Fennema, A.C., 63
Figueroa, R.A., 74
Finkel, D., 76
Fox, P.W., 21, 37, 38, 39, 65
Frieman, J., 21, 37, 38
Frith, U., 27

Gabrieli, J.D.E., 63
Gilmore, D., 81
Glick, M.J., 21, 48, 114, 153
Goldstein, A.G., 91
Goldstein, L.H., 25
Gordon, J.H., 63
Gordon, P., 21, 30, 103, 127
Grafman, J., 69
Gray, C.R., 21, 48, 114, 152, 153
Grierson, M., 10
Groom, D., 90
Gummerman, K., 21, 48, 114, 152, 153

Haber, R.N., 5
Hall, V.C., 75
Hamilton, G., 75
Hampson, P., 89
Hancock, J., 117
Hanggi, D., 81
Hanley, J.R., 64, 65, 68
Harrison, J., 25
Harshman, R., 32, 101

Hasher, L., 91
Hawkins, S., 74
Hayman, C.A.G., 63
Haywood, M.C., 78
Heal, L.H., 78
Heath, P., 65
Heckhausen, J., 36
Hegge, T., 12
Heindel, W.C., 63
Hennelly, R.A., 45
Hermelin, B., 49
Hernstadt, R., 78
Hishitani, S., 82
Hitch, G.J., 51
Holevas, A., 49, 51
Hoosain, R., 45
Humphreys, G.W., 65
Hunt, E.B., 21, 27, 30, 75, 76, 81, 127
Hunter, I.M.L., 3, 10, 21, 29, 30, 132

Imreh, G., 51
Ingham, J.G., 69, 71, 77, 154
Intons-Peterson, M.J., 52
Isaac, A.R., 82

Jakobson, R., 25
Jarrell, G.R., 76
Jensen, A.R., 74
Johnson, S., 21, 42, 43, 44
Jones, H.E., 10
Jones, S., 89
Judd, T., 49
Jurden, F.H., 74
Just, M.A., 74

Kanner, L., 27
Kaplan, E., 49, 51
Kapur, N., 65
Kaye, B., 74
Keane, M.M., 63
Kelly, S.W., 78
Kennedy, P., 65
Kent, R.D., 48
Klausmeier, H.J., 78
Kliegl, R., 36, 82
Knowlton, B., 63

Knyazeva, G.R., 65
Kyllonen, P., 74

Landis, T., 65
Lang, A.E., 63
Lashley, K.S., 69
Leavitt, L.A., 48
Lee, S-Y., 45
Leslie, A.M., 27
Levine, D.N., 65
Lewis, J., 75
Liker, J.K., 76, 78
Lindenberger, U., 82
Liotti, M., 65
Lockhart, R.S., 69
Loftus, E.F., 76
Lorayne, H., 59
Lord, A.B., 2
Love, T., 21, 27, 30, 127
Lucci, D., 49, 51
Lunneborg, C., 75
Luria, A.R., 3, 21, 22, 132

Macdonald, C.A., 63
Mackintosh, N., 74
MacLeod, C.M., 81
Mahadevan, R.S., 21, 37, 38, 39, 65
Malhotra, D., 81
Manturzewska, M., 51
Marks, D.F., 82
Marschark, M., 82
Massaro, D.W., 48
Mathews, N.N., 81
McGeorge, P., 78
McGue, M., 76
McKelvie, S.J., 81, 89
Meudell, P., 65
Miklazewski, K., 51
Miller, L.K., 49
Miller, L.T., 75
Mishkin, M., 65
Mohindra, N.,K., 90
Mohr, G., 80
Morris, P.E., 89
Morton, J.A., 41
Moscovitch, M., 63

Moss, M.B., 66, 69, 154
Mukunda, K.V., 75
Müller, G., 12, 13, 14
Musen, G., 63

Nadel, L., 65, 69, 70
Neisser, U., 81, 87
Nelson, K., 70
Nettelbeck, T., 79
Newcombe, F., 65
Newell, A., 76
Nichelli, N., 65
Noice, H., 53
Noice, T., 53
Novoa, L., 21, 47, 152

O'Brien, D., 10, 117
O'Connor, M., 80
O'Connor, N., 49
O'Keefe, J., 65
Obler, L.K., 21, 22, 47, 152
Ohta, N., 63
Oliver, W.L., 52
Osborn, H.F., 52
Ostergard, A.L., 63, 64

Paivio, A., 32, 82, 101
Pallis, C.A., 65
Palmer, E.P., 65
Park, C.C., 49
Payne, M., 66, 69, 154
Pearson, N.A., 65
Pedersen, N., 76
Perruchet, P., 63
Plomin, R., 76
Polson, P.G., 21, 36, 57
Powers, P.A., 76
Psotka, J., 49, 152, 153, 156

Quast, Z., 89
Quintilian, 9

Rabbitt, P.M.A., 79, 148, 154
Rashid, W., 81
Ratcliff, G., 65
Reber, A.S., 64, 78

Reichard, G.A., 25
Restle, F., 69
Richardson, A., 81, 82, 159
Richardson, J.T.E., 80
Riddoch, M.J., 65
Rimland, B., 27
Rohwer, W.D., Jr., 82
Rose, S.P.R., 72
Rozin, P., 69
Rubin, D.C., 2
Rule, W.R., 76

Sadoski, M., 80
Saint-Cyr, J.A., 63
Salili, F., 45
Salmon, D.P., 63
Salthouse, T.A., 78
Sandberg, T., 75
Sandor, B., 19
Schacter, D.L., 61, 63
Schweizer, K., 75
Seamon, J.G., 65
Sheehan, P.W., 81
Shell, P., 74
Shepard, R.N., 5
Simon, H.A., 58
Sinnamon, H.M., 65
Sloboda, J.A., 49
Smith, J., 36
Smyth, M.M., 52
Sperling, G., 48
Squire, L.R., 63
Stake, R.E., 77
Standing, L., 5
Starkes, J.L., 53
Stevenson, H., 45
Stigler, J., 45
Stratton, G., 2

Stromeyer, C.F., 49, 152, 153, 156
Surian, L., 82
Susukita, T., 14

Tanwar, U., 81
Taylor, A.E., 63
Thompson, C.P., 21, 37, 38
Thorndyke, P.W., 111
Tresch, M.C., 65
Tulving, E., 61, 63

Ungeleider, L.G., 65

Valentine, E., 21, 22, 30, 81, 96, 98,
    103, 105, 127
Vernon, P.A., 75
Vogl, R.J., 21, 37, 38

Walkenfeld, F.F., 78
Warach, J., 65
Warren, E., 90
Waterhouse, L., 49
Weingartner, H., 69
Weinland, J.D., 19
Weiskrantz, L., 66
Werth, E., 25
Wicinski, A.A., 51
Wilding, J., 21, 22, 30, 81, 96, 98, 103,
    105, 127
Wilson, B., 65
Witherspoon, D., 63
Wood, F.B., 26
Wyke, M.A., 25

Yates, F.A., 9
Young, A.W., 64, 65, 68

Zacks, R.T., 91

Subject Index

Actors, 51–53
Age, 79, 148
Aitken, 3, 29–30
Amnesia/amnesic syndrome, 66, 70
Ampäre, 10
Arnould, 12
Asperger's syndrome, 27
Association/associations, 13–14, 18, 20, 24, 27, 28, 29, 32, 59, 60, 106, 109, 132
Atkinson-Shiffrin (keeping track) task, 30–31
Autism, 27, 49–50
Autobiographical recall, 70, 159

Backward spelling, 48–49
Ballet dancers, 53
Brain damage, 64–67
Bubbles, P., 42–44
Buxton, Jedediah, 10

Calendrical calculation, 107
Cards, playing, 43–44, 109, 118
Carvello, Creighton, 118
Chess, 73
Chunks, 34, 41
CJ, 47–48, 49, 56, 57
Coding/recoding, 12, 18, 29, 34–35, 156
Combinatorial binding model, 70
Conceptual peg, 132
Control group, details of, 95–98

Correlational studies, 67–69, 71
Criteria for natural memory ability, 4, 137–138

Datas, 10
DD, 33
Declarative memory, 61–62
Diamandi, 12
Digits, digit matrix, digit span, 5, 11–14, 17–21, 22, 29, 33–35, 38–43, 45–47, 90, 103–107, 127–128, 131, 160

Earliest memory, 26–27, 82, 105, 112, 125–126, 146
    detail in, 125, 146–147, 159
Ebbinghaus, 13
ED, 100–101
Eidetic imagery, 6, 17, 20, 49, 105
Elly, 49
Encoding, 4, 20, 25, 66, 79, 82, 136, 148–149, 157
Episodic memory, 61–65, 70
Explicit memory, 62–63, 78
Euler, 10
Everyday memory, 5

Face–name task, 3–4, 89
Faces/face recognition, 88–89, 148
Factor analysis, 67–68, 146–149, 157
Family, see Relatives

Figure alphabet, 31–32, 132
Finkelstein, 19–20
Free recall, 89

Gauss, 10
General memory ability, 7, 27, 44, 61,
  68, 70–71, 137, 143, 147–148, 157

Hancock, Jonathan, 1, 117

Image/imagery, *see also* Eidetic
  imagery, 13, 18, 20, 22–23, 26, 32,
  43, 80–83, 104–105, 109, 112–113,
  127–128, 160
Implicit memory, 62–64, 78
Inaudi, 11–12
Incidental learning, 30
Individual Differences Questionnaire
  (IDQ), 32, 101, 113, 128–9, 160
Intelligence, 11, 73–80, 148, 159–160
Ishihara, 14–19

JC, 36–37
JD, 49
JR, 6, 103–105, 114, 121

K, 10–11
Kasparov, G., 73
KC, 98, 100

Language, 47–48, 49
Learning ability, 77
Locale system, 65, 69
Loci, method of, 2, 9, 23, 35, 118, 130,
  132
Long-term memory, 61–73, 76

Macaulay, Thomas, 10–11
Mahadevan, Rajan Srinivasan, 3,
  37–41
Meaning, 24, 27, 39, 53, 111, 154
Messiaen, 25
Methods, *see* Strategies
Mill Hill Vocabulary Scale, 97, 103,
  128, 146, 148, 159–160
Mnemonic methods, *see* Strategies

Modularity, 61–69, 72, 135–136,
  151–153
Motivation, 4, 19, 41, 113
Music, 50–51

Names, 60, 90, 107
Natural memory ability, 5–7, 27, 104,
  114, 155–158
'Naturals', 136–142
Neurobiology, 72–73
Nonsense syllables, 12–13, 30–31
Non-strategic tasks, 138–140
Numbers, *see* Digits

O'Brien, Dominic, 1, 14, 33, 117–118

Parallel distributed processing
  (PDP), 71–72
Paul, 49
Perceptual representation system
  (PRS), 63–65
Pi, memorisation of, 40–41, 130
Pictures, 5, 48, 91
Poetry, 2, 24
Practice, 30–39, 50–51, 56–58
Prime ministers, memory for, 90, 125,
  146
Procedural memory, 61–62

Rajan, *see* Mahadevan
Ramanujan, Srinivasa, 40
Relatives, 138, 141, 159
Retention, 4, 17, 26, 30, 71, 77, 79,
  100, 104, 110, 133–134, 136–140,
  144–146, 148, 154
Retrieval, 4, 66–67, 71
Retrieval structure, 33–35
Rhythm, 29
Rimbaud, 25
Rote memorisation, 28, 35, 52
Routes, 49
RR, 100
Rückle, Dr, 12–14

Saints-Saens, 4
Self-reports, 58–59

Semantic memory, 61–62, 70
SF, 33–36
Shereshevskii (S.), 3, 22–27, 42–43, 59
Simonides, 2
Skilled memory theory, 35–36, 53, 58–60
Snow-crystals, 91, 94–95
Spatial–temporal position, 91–93
Specificity/specific memory factors, 7, 44, 61–71, 151–154
Speed of processing, 78–79
Speed-up, 35–36
Storage, *see* Retention
Stories, 32, 49, 87–88, 111–112
Strategic memory, 114
Strategic tasks, 138–140
Strategies, 5, 7, 16–18, 20–21, 23, 32–33, 47, 56–60, 107, 113, 129–133, 138, 151–152, 155, 158
Strategists, 136–142
Surface processing, 24–25, 27–28
Synaesthesia, 24–26, 106

Tasks, 21, 27, 30, 46, 84, 95, 118
Taxons, 65
TE, 30–33, 42–43, 59, 127–128
Techniques, *see* Strategies
TM, 105–114, 127–128
Tomoyori, Hideaki, 3, 37
Tovey, Donald Francis, 10
Toscanini, 4
Transfer-appropriate processing account, 63

Visual memory, 48–49, 68, 130
Vividness of Visual Imagery Questionnaire (VVIQ), 103, 113, 129, 160
VP, 27–29, 42–43, 59, 127–128

Welch, Leslie, 10–11, 132
Words, 89–90
Working memory, 61, 68, 74–75
World Memory Championships, 1, 117

Zander, 4